"A bold, yet wise approach to the core problems of depersonalization. This scientifically sound combination of acceptance and behavioral approaches can fundamentally change the life direction of people struggling with this debilitating disorder. Highly recommended."

—Steven C. Hayes, Ph.D., Foundation Professor of Psychology at the University of Nevada and author of *Get Out of Your Mind and Into Your Life*

Overcoming

Depersonalization

Disorder

a mindfulness & acceptance guide to
conquering feelings of numbness & unreality

FUGEN NEZIROGLU, PH.D.
KATHARINE DONNELLY, MA

New Harbinger Publications, Inc.

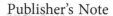

Publisher's Note

Care has been taken to confirm the accuracy of the information presented and to describe generally accepted practices. However, the authors, editors, and publisher are not responsible for errors or omissions or for any consequences from application of the information in this book and make no warranty, express or implied, with respect to the contents of the publication.

The authors, editors, and publisher have exerted every effort to ensure that any drug selection and dosage set forth in this text are in accordance with current recommendations and practice at the time of publication. However, in view of ongoing research, changes in government regulations, and the constant flow of information relating to drug therapy and drug reactions, the reader is urged to check the package insert for each drug for any change in indications and dosage and for added warnings and precautions. This is particularly important when the recommended agent is a new or infrequently employed drug.

Some drugs and medical devices presented in this publication may have Food and Drug Administration (FDA) clearance for limited use in restricted research settings. It is the responsibility of the health care provider to ascertain the FDA status of each drug or device planned for use in their clinical practice.

Distributed in Canada by Raincoast Books

Copyright © 2010 by Fugen Neziroglu & Katharine Donnelly
New Harbinger Publications, Inc.
5674 Shattuck Avenue
Oakland, CA 94609
www.newharbinger.com

FSC
Mixed Sources
Product group from well-managed
forests and other controlled sources
Cert no. SW-COC-002283
www.fsc.org
© 1996 Forest Stewardship Council

Acquired by Catharine Sutker; Cover design by Amy Shoup;
Edited by Nelda Street; Text design by Tracy Marie Carlson

Library of Congress Cataloging-in-Publication Data

Neziroglu, Fugen A., 1951-
  Overcoming depersonalization disorder : a mindfulness and acceptance guide to conquering feelings of numbness and unreality / Fugen Neziroglu and Katharine Donnelly ; foreword by Daphne Simeon.
     p. cm.
  Includes bibliographical references.
  ISBN 978-1-57224-706-2
  1. Depersonalization. I. Donnelly, Katherine Fair. II. Title.
  RC553.D4N49 2010
  616.89'142--dc22

                                        2010009307

12 11 10

10 9 8 7 6 5 4 3 2 1   First printing

Contents

Foreword

Overcoming Depersonalization Disorder, by Fugen Neziroglu, Katharine Donnelly, and Jose Yaryura-Tobias, is a very welcome addition to the scant book literature on depersonalization disorder. Although the disorder is estimated to afflict up to 2 percent of people over the course of their lifetimes, it remains underdiagnosed and frequently misdiagnosed, leaving its sufferers increasingly frustrated and hopeless as they go from one mental health professional to the next looking for an accurate diagnosis, effective treatment, and hope for the future. Even when the disorder is accurately diagnosed, many clinicians remain at a loss as to how to best treat these patients, since the treatment guidelines for chronic depersonalization continue to be obscure compared to those for many other psychiatric disorders. This new book, happily, offers a wealth of psychological treatment approaches that can ultimately prove helpful to many people afflicted by the disorder.

The book is highly readable, targeting a lay audience as well as clinicians looking for informed help in treating their patients. In the first three chapters, the book introduces all the intricate aspects of the condition, including its symptoms; its course over time; its common antecedents, such as trauma and family dysfunction; and, importantly, its overlap with and its differences from related psychiatric disorders. This book also covers some basic neurobiology in order to give the reader a solid sense of what we know about the biological underpinnings of the disorder.

The bulk of the book is dedicated to a wide variety of psychotherapy approaches that can be used to tackle chronic depersonalization. Its unique contribution is the fact that it draws from both acceptance and commitment therapy and dialectical behavior therapy, and specifically applies both of these models to the treatment of depersonalization. The authors describe in simple and clear ways, illustrated by many examples, how self-focus and obsessional preoccupation with the illness often brings more suffering, while a mental stance based on mindfulness in the moment and on acceptance as a contextual background to the work of change can alleviate pain and suffering. The book describes thoughts, feelings, and avoidance behaviors that stem from the condition and exacerbate it, with an emphasis on enhancing the person's growth potential and commitment to valued aspects of life even in the face of very distressing symptoms.

The authors then introduce basic principles of dialectical behavior therapy as they apply to chronic depersonalization: present-moment mindfulness, distress tolerance, awareness and regulation of emotions, and interpersonal effectiveness. These are supplemented with classic behavioral approaches focusing on exposure and response prevention, targeting not only the symptoms of depersonalization but also its historical precipitants and its most feared outcomes. The book ends with some additional treatment options such as cognitive approaches, general wellness strategies, and an overview of pharmacological treatment options.

This is a comprehensive, up-to-date, highly readable, and user-friendly book. It offers many vignettes and examples, exercises and worksheets, helpful concluding summaries to each chapter, and a question-and-answer section addressing some of the most frequently expressed concerns of people with depersonalization disorder. It is a very welcome addition to a newly emerging field, and one that patients and clinicians alike will find very helpful.

—Daphne Simeon, MD
 author of *Feeling Unreal: Depersonalization Disorder
 and the Loss of Self*
 Associate Professor of Psychiatry Beth Israel Medical Center
 and Albert Einstein College of Medicine New York

Acknowledgments

This book was inspired by our work with a few people who moved us with their overwhelming suffering and ultimate resilience. Depersonalization disorder (DPD) is one of many psychological conditions that don't fit comfortably into one category. Depersonalization might describe an obsessive-compulsive process, a symptom of somatization or hypochondriasis, an extension of panic disorder or post-traumatic stress disorder, an extreme of depression, or really any other form of extreme suffering. However, DPD might instead manifest as numbness, "fogginess," social alienation, or similar complaints. Because DPD tends to mess with your very sense of self and awareness, it's one of the more disturbing of the somatization/anxiety disorders. We would especially like to acknowledge those of you with DPD for sharing the stories of your struggles, the stories that pepper this book.

We would also like to acknowledge the tireless clinicians and researchers who have contributed to the empirical foundation for this book. Daphne Simeon, MD; Dawn Baker, D.Clin.Psy.; Elaine Hunter, Ph.D.; Nicholas Medford, M.R.C.Psych.; Emma J. Lawrence, B.Sc., Ph.D.; and Anthony S. David, MD, F.R.C.Psych., have established the framework for contemporary research on depersonalization and other dissociative conditions. Steven C. Hayes, Ph.D.; Kelly G. Wilson, Ph.D.; Kirk D. Strosahl, Ph.D.; Michael P. Twohig, Ph.D.; Jon Kabat-Zinn, Ph.D.; and Marsha Linehan, Ph.D., have provided the research and philosophy that have fueled and given credit to the acceptance-oriented therapeutic movement, which has inspired this book's therapeutic emphasis.

We would also like to acknowledge the publishers who have worked relentlessly to make this a user-friendly manual. Specifically, Catharine Sutker has provided us with needed guidance and constant feedback. She has been invaluable in her encouragement and support with this and previous books.

Finally, we would like to acknowledge the support of our friends and family members.

Introduction

My friends and family don't understand what I go through.
My parents always say, "You're crying now. How can you
say you can't feel anything?" Whenever I try to explain,
I just feel I'm coming across as defensive. What's the use?
People in my life will never understand me. How can they?
They never felt depersonalized, isolated from everything
around them, as if they were just going through the motions
of living. Who lives like a robot day in and day out? I feel
so anxious about my future and afraid I'll never be able
to change this horrible state of unreality. Everything seems

so far away, different from the way it used to look. What happened to me, to my brain? Why do I feel like this? Will it ever go away? I don't want to be around people: it's just too hard.

The quote above, which a young woman with depersonalization disorder (DPD) provided, highlights a common experience among people with depersonalization: most people in your life don't understand what depersonalization feels like or how much it makes you suffer. Unfortunately, this includes loved ones and mental health professionals alike. You've probably picked up this book because these frustrations are all too familiar to you. Maybe you've been down an often-fruitless path as you sought help from the mental health care system. Perhaps you've received misdiagnoses and tried countless medications, as you try to feel normal again.

If you are like most people with chronic depersonalization, when you finally came across the term "depersonalization," you were probably very moved to hear that others feel as you do and that you finally found a word that describes your experience. Yet, maybe you've never heard other people talk about their own experiences with depersonalization. Some psychological terms are part of the public vocabulary; if you tell a friend or family member you had a panic attack, that person will generally understand what this means before you describe your experience. Depersonalization isn't as familiar to most people, which means that not only do you have the pressure to "get better," but you also have to explain yourself and educate other people about the condition. You may also have to take the initiative for your own treatment. Finding a psychiatrist or psychologist who specializes in treating depression, phobias, or borderline personality disorder may be simple enough, but finding a mental health professional with an expertise in treating depersonalization disorder isn't always as easy. Fortunately, more and more people are gradually becoming interested in depersonalization disorder.

Research into depersonalization is still in a formative stage, so relative to other psychological phenomena, we have a lot to learn about it. But one thing is clear for the time being: there's no quick fix, and there are no infallible medical options. If you have a bacterial infection and take antibiotics for it, it's likely to go away. Depersonalization doesn't respond in this way. The fact is, there's no cure for depersonalization disorder, and searching for a way out of it may even do more harm than good. This may be difficult for you to hear, but at the same time, we want you to know that there are things you can do to feel better. DPD is treatable, and you can get your life back. The purpose of this guide is to help you manage your discomfort while staying engaged in life. We'll explore principles of acceptance and provide strategies that will help you tolerate your discomfort on a daily basis while pursuing what's important to you. This is essential, because ultimately, beating depersonalization means refusing to let it push you around and dictate how you'll live your life. While we can't promise a *cure* for depersonalization, we can arm you with an approach and a plan that will allow you to take back the reins. And while it's not your fault that you ended up in this situation, you are the only one who can start the process of moving forward. We believe that no one with depersonalization is doomed to a half-life, and while recovery is a difficult process, it's not a hopeless one.

The first half of this book will give you more information about depersonalization and DPD. The later chapters will focus on treatment. We'll introduce acceptance and commitment therapy (ACT) and show you how you can use it to suffer less and live a better life—even *with* depersonalization. We'll also introduce mindfulness and grounding strategies, along with other dialectical behavior therapy exercises. Finally, we'll teach behavioral strategies to help you confront your discomfort and pursue healthy, functional life activities.

Assumptions of This Book

As we approach the task of helping you manage depersonalization, we assume the following about you—and all people, for that matter. It's important that you keep these assumptions in mind as you learn the behavioral and acceptance strategies we'll discuss later on:

- There's nothing inherently *wrong* with you. Your mind has actually found an important and adaptive way of dealing with the unique obstacles life may have thrown your way. As we'll explain in chapter 3, when you developed depersonalization, you may have preferred numbness to feeling what you would have otherwise felt.

- Your feelings are very important. You have suffered a great deal, and your pain informs us that feeling connected to people and your environment is important to you. If you are miserable because you can't tap into your feelings anymore, it's because human connectedness is very important to you. As we'll discuss in greater detail in chapter 6, it's important to be willing to experience your pain, because it represents the flip side of what you value the most.

- Having respect for your feelings doesn't necessarily mean acting the way they urge you to do. Even though your feelings are there to protect you, they sometimes pressure you to do things that aren't in your best interest. As you'll see in chapters 6 and 7, mindfulness strategies can help you listen to your thoughts and feelings while acting in a deliberate manner, with attention to what actions are actually in your best interest.

- It's impossible to entirely avoid suffering if you are doing anything of value. Love is inherently peppered with disappointment, conflict, and loss; professional advancement requires sacrifice, energy expenditure, and patience; friendships entail selflessness and investment. Nothing worth pursuing is painless, and that includes using the strategies in this book to cope with depersonalization. Expect that this will be a difficult process, and try to keep your focus on how much you value getting better: even though it's painful, what about this process is worthwhile to you?

- The present moment is all you have to work with. Although it's easy to become preoccupied with past failures or future worries, now is the only thing that's real. The acceptance and mindfulness strategies we'll explore throughout this book will help you keep your focus on the present moment.

How to Use This Book

This book is designed to help you understand and overcome DPD. You can skim through the chapters to get an overall understanding of the basic concepts discussed, then go back and read each chapter more carefully. Of course, you won't identify with everything, because nobody experiences exactly the same symptoms, but there are bound to be things you can relate to, especially in the personal accounts of those who have DPD.

As you go through the book, be sure to take notes, complete the exercises, and follow the suggestions given. It will probably be helpful if your family members also read this book, so they can better understand how you feel. Chapter 7 will cover how to assertively communicate your experience to your loved ones, because sharing your experiences with, and being understood by, your loved ones will help decrease your feelings of isolation.

1

What Is Depersonalization?
What Is DPD?

Most people have unknowingly felt depersonalized at some point in their lives. We have all, at times, felt detached from ourselves, as if we were watching our lives as spectators. Maybe after a loved one passed away, you felt that all that used to be familiar was now foreign to you. The person accepting condolences from others, muttering appreciation and shaking hands, was some robotic, empty creature performing actions on your behalf, while you pondered the reason for existence. Or perhaps the events of September 11,

2001, rocked you to your core, causing you to feel disconnected from others, as if you were living in a nightmare. Feelings like this are common after tragedies such as natural disasters or a death in the family, and, for most people, go away as naturally as they came.

Yet it's likely that you've started reading this book not because you experience fleeting depersonalization during tragedy but, rather, because these experiences have spilled over into your every waking moment. You may wake up every day to an alarm clock, eat your breakfast, go to work, and interact with your family without an ounce of emotion, ambition, or true mental involvement. Maybe you have to pinch the skin on your leg to make sure that it does, in fact, belong to your body. Words that you hear every day may seem unfamiliar, common objects foreign, and your own children distant. Your world may feel unreal and dreamlike, as if your body were performing actions without your volition.

What Is Depersonalization?

Because 50 to 70 percent of people would say they have experienced depersonalization at some point in their lives, experiencing depersonalization doesn't necessarily mean you have a psychological disorder (Dixon 1963). However, *depersonalization disorder (DPD)*, a chronic experience of this common human phenomenon, is estimated to occur in only about 2 percent of the population (Sierra 2008). According to the *Diagnostic and Statistical Manual of Mental Disorders* (*DSM-IV-TR*) (APA 2000) (the reference mental health providers use to diagnose mental disorders), the following experiences define depersonalization disorder:

- You have persistent or recurrent feelings of being detached from your mental processes or body, as if you were merely an observer.

- Your experience of depersonalization causes significant distress and impairment in your social, work, or other functioning.

To be diagnosed with DPD, *reality testing* must be intact; that is, if you are experiencing depersonalization, you are aware that your experiences are unusual. In other words, you aren't hallucinating; you are aware of everything that's going on around you. Reality testing merely means that you have awareness and haven't lost touch with reality. Are you aware of the numbness, the lack of connectedness, the way your body feels, and how you think? If so, though you may not like what you are experiencing, you do have awareness. Also, for a diagnosis of DPD, depersonalization can't be the result of another disorder, substance use, or a general medical condition. Based on these criteria, if you believe you might have DPD, it's important to get confirmation from a mental health professional. Also, because psychological disorders can sometimes come in pairs, trios, or even quartets, diagnosis is best left to the professionals. An experienced mental health professional can help you figure out exactly what's going on, considering the whole picture.

Depersonalization may feel like being encapsulated in a bubble, as if you can't experience what's around you. You may feel as if you're on autopilot, or as if some unknown force has taken control of your body and it now acts independently of you. Depersonalization numbs you mentally and emotionally: you may feel that you go about your daily life without any true emotional connection, even regarding your spouse and children. You may not care about your actions or behaviors, while still having an understanding that you *should* care about such things. Naturally, a low mood, depression, anxiety, and increased worry can sometimes follow in the footsteps of depersonalization. It's quite distressing to feel so isolated from yourself and the world.

Depersonalization affects your mental processing. You may find it difficult to concentrate, feeling as if your mind has gone blank. On the other hand, your thoughts may be jumbled and confused, and you might have trouble retaining new information. Memories from your past may not seem like your own but someone else's, or they may simply seem very distant. You may also have trouble remembering everyday things.

The descriptions just mentioned are only a few of the many experiences of someone with depersonalization disorder. Later, we'll go into depth about these and other symptoms.

What Is Derealization?

Akin to depersonalization is derealization. Whereas depersonalization refers to an altered perception of yourself, *derealization*, a term coined in 1935 by Irish psychiatrist Edward Mapother (Mathew et al. 1999), refers to perceiving your environment in an altered way, and it's often a manifestation of DPD. People experiencing derealization describe it as seeing the external world as strange or unreal. For example, your vision may be distorted so that objects appear larger or smaller than they really are. A familiar scene may seem foreign or somehow perverted. Objects in the environment may seem as if they're somehow not the same as you know them to be, as though they're not the right size or shape, or as if they're alien in some other way.

Throughout this book, we'll refer to four people with DPD whom the authors have worked with. Emily, a young woman with depersonalization disorder, always acknowledged being overwhelmed by her environment. She said she couldn't read because she couldn't focus on the individual words but, instead, became distracted by the whole picture. John, who also has DPD, said that when he closed his eyes, he had the sensation that the chair he was sitting in was way too small for him, that the bed he was lying in was engulfing him, or that the room he was in was caving in on him. He knew intellectually that the environment wasn't *really* changing; therefore, what he was experiencing was derealization rather than hallucination. Both Emily and John were experiencing symptoms of derealization associated with DPD.

Derealization may also cause you to question the purpose of things in your everyday environment. For example, you might feel that cars on the street move without purpose. The people with whom you interact on a regular basis may seem unfamiliar to you or mechanical. Because the world around you appears unreal or artificial, you might experience unusual physical and perceptual sensations and have sensations of weightlessness or loss of basic senses (such as smell, touch, or taste). You may experience feelings of being slowed down or sped up. Objects may seem two-dimensional or less colorful. Dizziness is also common. Your own voice may even sound distant or unfamiliar to you. Basically, your experience of everything you can observe (including your own internal sensations) may be distorted.

QUIZ:
Do You Have Symptoms of Depersonalization?

1. Do you feel hollow inside?

2. Do you feel as if you've lost your sense of self?

3. Do you feel as if you are observing yourself from the outside, looking inside?

4. Do you feel like a robot?

5. Are you numb, unable to feel emotions, although you know what you are supposed to feel?

6. Would you describe your experience as the life of the "living dead"?

7. Does the world around you seem strange, as if you don't perceive it as others do?

8. Do your body and mind seem disconnected?

9. Does everything around you seem foggy or unreal?

10. Are you living in a dream world where everything's surreal?

11. Are you an actor onstage, knowing your part but not feeling it?

12. Do you spend a lot of time thinking about philosophical or religious issues (such as why we exist, whether we actually exist, who's really talking, and what time and space really are)?

13. Does your thinking seem separate from your body?

14. Are you paying a lot of attention to your bodily sensations, your thoughts, or both?

15. Do you fear that you're not controlling your own actions?

16. Are you overly aware of noise?

17. Do objects look different than before?

18. Do you feel as if there's an inner voice that's yours but that simultaneously converses with you and interrupts your other thoughts?

19. Do you feel detached from things and people around you?

20. Do you feel as if you are in a constant state of detachment?

If you identify with even half of these questions, it's possible that you have depersonalization disorder. Yet, to know for sure, it's important that you consult a mental health professional who has some experience working with DPD and other dissociative disorders.

When Does DPD Happen?

DPD isn't always a severe or persistent problem; for some people, the feeling lasts hours, days, weeks, or months. For others, it's a lifelong struggle. Still others have symptoms of DPD after a severe psychological or emotional experience, such as a loss. This is why it can be rather complicated to actually receive a diagnosis of DPD. Because some overlap exists between symptoms of DPD and major depressive disorder (MDD) or generalized anxiety disorder (GAD), DPD is often misdiagnosed. Researchers have found that approximately two-thirds of people who survived life-threatening danger remember symptoms of DPD at the time of their trauma (Cardeña and Spiegel 1993), suggesting that depersonalization may be a strategy the brain uses to cope with trauma.

DPD can cause severe anxiety; at the same time, anxiety can also lead to depersonalization. Severe and lasting symptoms of DPD are often seen in people with agoraphobia (fear of public places), hypochondriasis (health anxiety), or obsessive-compulsive disorder (OCD, which is characterized by intrusive thoughts called obsessions, compulsions to act on them, or both). We'll discuss the relationship between DPD and other disorders in greater detail in chapter 4.

Interestingly, those who have used drugs may be particularly vulnerable to DPD. In fact, some people say that their symptoms began immediately after illicit drug use. We'll discuss the relationship between DPD and drug use in chapter 3.

Because of similarities between DPD and other disorders, you may have received diagnoses that didn't exactly address the issue that causes you so much discomfort. Even the psychologists and psychiatrists you've consulted for help may not have been able to understand what's wrong with you, which may have contributed to your frustration and alienation. Since dissociative symptoms are difficult to define objectively, people who don't experience such symptoms may doubt the disorder's validity. It's undeniable, however, that depersonalization exists. As a scientific understanding of DPD continues to develop and as our understanding of this condition increases, mental health professionals will become better able to identify and treat it.

Behaviors, Feelings, and Thoughts Associated with DPD

Earlier, we described some of the symptoms of DPD, but now let's take a closer look. Let's break those symptoms into five experiential factors. See if you think any of the following describes you.

Sensory Changes:

- Things don't taste or smell the same as before.

- Objects look farther away or nearer.

- Your world seems brighter.

Perceptual Changes:

- Your voice seems altered in some way.

- You feel unreal.

- You feel as if you live in a dreamworld.

Mood Changes:

- You feel anxious.

- You feel depressed.

- You are numb.

- You are emotionally detached.

Changes in How You Think:

- Your thoughts don't seem to belong to you.

- You are confused.

- You are always trying to figure out what went wrong with your brain.

Behavioral Changes:

- You are disorganized.

- You are distracted and seem distant in conversations.

- You have difficulty following through on a task.

If you identified with any of these symptoms and found that you answered yes to most of the questions on the quiz, this book may help you. DPD can disrupt your life and make you feel very alone and isolated. Often people with DPD feel very misunderstood and can't explain what they're going through. You may feel as if you speak a different language from everyone else around you. Next we will explore how these symptoms may get in the way in life.

How Does DPD Affect Your Life?

DPD can interfere with so many areas of your daily functioning. Foremost, you probably feel disorganized and confused. Your concentration and ability to achieve your goals may seem directly related to how "depersonalized" you feel. DPD makes it difficult to focus and get going. Everything seems to take more time.

Notice whether you avoid doing things that make you uncomfortable. For example, do you find yourself avoiding going out shopping or to certain bars or restaurants because you find the noise level intolerable? Do you drive only short distances because things seem far away and driving feels hazardous? Are you just uncomfortable in your own skin and therefore keep checking the mirror or other reflective surfaces to get a grip on yourself? Maybe instead of looking at yourself, you pinch yourself to make sure you can feel. Is going to school or work getting more difficult? You may find that socializing takes a tremendous amount of effort.

EXERCISE: How My DPD Interferes with My Life

Take a minute to list the ways your DPD interferes with your life, and let's see if, by the end of this book, you've been able to change some of those behaviors.

1. _____

2. _____

3. _____

4. _____

5. _____

6. _____

7. _____

8. _____

When You Need Professional Help

You may be wondering whether DPD is something you can tackle on your own or whether you need someone, such as a mental health professional, to help you. This is no easy question to answer, but three rules of thumb apply to seeking treatment for just about every psychological disorder. Definitely seek treatment if you are suffering severely, have lost functioning in some important area of your life, or have had any suicidal feelings or thoughts. When in doubt, it's best to go to a qualified therapist.

When seeking treatment, make sure to find a therapist who practices behavior therapy. In the following chapters we'll explore the reasons why behavior therapy is the way to go for treatment of depersonalization. But for now, just remember, when you speak with prospective therapists, don't be afraid to ask questions; for example, ask whether they have ever treated anyone with depersonalization disorder and whether they practice exposure and response prevention, as well as behavioral activation, techniques we'll explain in chapter 8. If you do seek treatment, keep in mind that in addition to having a behavioral orientation, the best therapist for you will be someone you'll bond with. So look for someone with a warm disposition, who has empathy for what you're going through.

Depersonalization as a Dissociative Disorder

Depersonalization is only one of the *dissociative disorders* identified in the *DSM-IV-TR* (APA 2000). *Dissociation* means partial or total lack of awareness about some aspect of your experiences. In other words, it means that in some way, you don't have access to the present moment. As we've explored, depersonalization involves a numbing to your internal experiences, whether this relates to your emotions, your feelings about certain people, your sensations, or your attention; some aspect of your experience is inaccessible or dulled. But depersonalization is only one of the experiences described as dissociative. Most people have heard about *dissociative identity disorder* (*DID*, which previously was commonly known as *multiple-* or *split-personality disorder*), which basically involves the development of one or more "alter egos," or distinct personalities. People who are diagnosed with DID seem to be so significantly dissociated that they no longer have one unified consciousness. People with DID generally have no awareness that they've slipped from one "alter" into another, and memories of behaviors carried out by one alter are forgotten by the others. Sometimes people with DID also say they experience depersonalization, but it generally doesn't work the other way around (people with DPD don't usually have alter egos).

Predictors of depersonalization and dissociative identity overlap (abuse and trauma, for example). But DID is typically associated with more significant trauma. So if daydreaming, depersonalization, and DID all lie on the same continuum, then daydreaming would be normal and common; brief depersonalization would be normal but infrequent; chronic depersonalization would be abnormal, nearly constant, and a sign of psychological dysfunction; and DID would be on the far end of the continuum: abnormal, dysfunctional, and relatively more destructive. While daydreaming and brief episodes of depersonalization may not be a psychological concern, chronic depersonalization and DID are very destructive and distressing.

DID is quite rare, and some controversy surrounds this diagnosis because the prevalence of this disorder is so much greater in the United States than the rest of the world. A possible explanation is that different cultures have different overall ways of dealing with emotions. For our purposes, it's enough to say that dissociation is real; it can come about in different ways, but it's a common way for human beings to respond to extreme stress or trauma. Other dissociative disorders include dissociative fugue and dissociative amnesia. While we don't have the space to elaborate further on DID, dissociative fugue, or dissociative amnesia, these conditions are fascinating, and many books (whether self-help books, information guides, or memoirs) exist concerning them. For example, *The Dissociative Identity Disorder Sourcebook*, by Deborah Haddock (McGraw-Hill, 2001), provides a user-friendly manual for people with DID as well as their families.

SUMMARY

As you can see, DPD can affect anyone, anytime. If you have any one of the symptoms mentioned, know that you're not alone; there are many people out there who suffer as you do. In this chapter, we reviewed symptoms and diagnostic criteria of DPD, and how DPD may affect your life. We broke the symptoms down into the different ways you can experience depersonalization and the different areas of life that are affected. In the following chapters, we'll start to approach the task of understanding and managing depersonalization symptoms.

2

Why You Can't Think Your
Way Out of DPD

In this chapter, we'll explore the immense impact of *self-focus* on DPD discomfort. Don't misunderstand; we're not referring to conceitedness, self-indulgence, self-pity, self-absorption, narcissism, selfishness, or any of the like. Self-focus means constant monitoring of internal sensations that heighten your sensitivity to the feeling of depersonalization. In other words, it's any internal experience—whether a thought, sensation, emotion, or memory—that makes you acknowledge your discomfort and the impact it may have on your life. Next we'll explore how self-focus leads to obsessive thinking about how to *get out* of the current feeling state. Obsessive self-focus may lead to an endless battle with unpleasant thoughts, frustration, and hopelessness. In this chapter we'll briefly introduce what might be the alternative to this relentless cycle, and as we progress in this book, we'll give you many practical strategies for ending the battle.

Self-Focus Makes Things Worse, Not Better

Depersonalization is a psychological "problem," and humans have a natural drive to solve problems. However, we're generally unable to permanently force changes in thoughts and feelings. If you could force feelings of depersonalization away with the same efficiency involved in taking out the garbage, you wouldn't be suffering. You wouldn't need this book, nor would you need medications or mental health treatment. It would be as simple as willing your experiences of depersonalization away. This conundrum of the human experience applies to many areas of suffering: it's hard to make yourself feel better when you're dealing with depression, social anxiety, bereavement, or disappointment, and efforts to change the way you feel generally don't work.

Furthermore, thinking about certain psychological problems and trying to feel better may actually make things worse. For example, if you are depressed and you reflect on the depression, you may imagine that depression will ruin your life; imagining in elaborate detail how painful every moment of your life will be if these feelings don't go away will make feelings of depression so much worse. Suddenly, depression is something to be depressed about. In the same way, thinking about feelings of depersonalization a lot also worsens them.

Suppose you wake up one day and nothing seems real, or your head feels incredibly foggy. Maybe you feel very far away; maybe you almost feel as though you are looking down on your experiences and actions as if they belong to someone else. At first, this may seem like a novel experience. Maybe it's also quite frightening, but at the onset of these feelings, you probably aren't focused on the possibility that they might not go away. You have probably not yet succumbed to despair about your predicament. Now flash forward a month into the future. Maybe you have gone to your general practitioner or family doctor, a psychologist, or a psychiatrist. Maybe you have been diagnosed with a number of other disorders that don't quite explain your symptoms, maybe someone has told you that you have depersonalization disorder, or maybe you have read personal accounts of this disorder on the Internet and discovered that, for some people, these feelings never go away.

Suddenly, your experiences become all the more unbearable. No longer do you simply have unpleasant experiences and sensations; suddenly you have a potentially lifelong condition. At this point, you would probably interpret sensations of depersonalization as totally awful, because not only are they unpleasant, they are also evidence of a chronic and debilitating condition. At that moment, your problem-solving brain is going to kick into overdrive. Your mind will become determined to escape discomfort and pursue any means to accomplish this. It's also at this moment that sensations of depersonalization are going to jump out at you because of what they imply about your overall psychological well-being. You start to worry about what the rest of your life will be like and how you're going to live with such horrific or dulled feelings. The symptoms are no longer merely uncomfortable because they're unpleasant; they are now uncomfortable because of what you believe they mean about how your life will be from this point on. You start to focus on your symptoms to the point of obsession, resulting in impairment and distress that's wedded to your most basic experiential faculties: your sensations, perceptions, thoughts, and emotional connectedness.

Obsession and Rumination

Two unpleasant ways of thinking tend to heighten self-focus: obsession and rumination. Everyone can become stuck on ideas or concerns, but obsession and rumination take getting stuck to the extreme. *Obsessions* are intrusive, forceful, or useless thoughts that become stuck in your mind. It's not always easy to see that your thoughts are obsessive; sometimes your thoughts may seem incredibly useful and urgent.

John frequently became so consumed by his thoughts that he often believed that there was something terribly wrong with his mind and body. He thought his doctors weren't capable of determining the cause of his symptoms, so he needed to do his homework to find a cause and a cure for his unpleasant feelings. He frequently returned to the idea that his symptoms must be related to some sort of systemic neurological degenerative process. He regularly requested that his therapists help him understand DPD again so he could accept the DPD diagnosis and relieve these obsessive thoughts. These thoughts were obsessive because they didn't lead him to any practical course of action but, rather, just to think the same things over and over again. The thoughts swirled around and around in his head, tightening their vice grip as he became more distressed.

Ruminations are similar. The word "rumination" comes from the description of a digestive process observed in cows and other grazing animals: the animal brings swallowed food up from its stomach in order to rechew it during rest. While a little disgusting, this is an illustrative metaphor. Basically, mental rumination refers to when the mind brings up unresolved issues to be mulled over and over and over again. It's more associated with chronic worry about *realistic* threats or sad thoughts (while obsessions aren't necessarily realistic).

For example, Susan frequently ruminated about her lack of feeling for her husband and children. Her thoughts circulated around this issue, exploring it from every angle again and again. The following excerpt was taken from a session with Susan, when she was asked to verbalize her thoughts in a free-associative manner:

> *I can't believe I don't feel love for him anymore. He was my only true concern for so many years, and I don't know what I'll do if I never get the feeling back. I sit and try to tap into it, but it's so abstract and confusing that it makes me sick. And what kind of mother doesn't feel anything for her children? A terrible mother. Everyone would be disgusted if they only knew what it feels like in here: when a mother doesn't care for her children, when a wife doesn't care for her husband. I feel sick.*

In some situations, self-focus and increased awareness of internal experiences does have a great benefit. For example, if you had some pain under your arms, this would not likely demand a lot of your attention. But if the pain didn't go away, you might eventually start ruminating about what could be wrong with you. You may not be able to push the sensation of this discomfort out of your mind. Suddenly, the possible *meaning* of discomfort exacerbates the discomfort you may feel. Now imagine that prolonged pain leads you to seek medical attention and you are given a diagnosis of lymphoma, a potentially deadly cancer. In this example, being aware of your symptoms may benefit you, because there are specific medical procedures that may cure you. Failure to acknowledge lymphoma symptoms will result in death. Therefore, obsessive awareness of sensations and what they mean is vital to your survival. On the other hand, many psychological conditions, including depersonalization, may get worse when you ruminate on them: thoughts about the condition and what this means for you will increase the presence of the symptoms and, in turn, make those sensations more prominent and distressing. And here's the irony of it: thinking about what you should do about it will generally not lead you to any resolution. So, while acknowledging lymphoma symptoms allows you to effectively solve health-related problems, obsessing about the symptoms of depersonalization merely leads to further anxiety and fear that the symptoms will always be there.

Susan described her self-focus and its impact this way:

My ability to tap into my feelings for my family has suffered. I sit and look at my husband, and will myself to feel what I used to about him. But I get caught up in that pursuit, and suddenly the feelings that were originally elusive become totally muddied by my thoughts. Suddenly, I wonder if it's even me who's thinking them. It's maddening. My thoughts sometimes feel like they're being generated by a computer, like I'm not even involved in my thoughts anymore.

Similarly, John related, "Obsession with my condition has crippled my thinking, and I'm constantly preoccupied with monitoring my feelings and sensations."

EXERCISE: How Have I Tried to "Solve" the "Problem" of Depersonalization?

Complete this exercise on a sheet of paper or in a notebook. Noting your experiences is very important to helping you understand how you may be increasing your distress. Also, keeping a written account on hand may help you notice when you're getting pulled into the fruitless war with your emotions.

1. Describe a situation where thinking about your feelings of depersonalization made you feel worse.

2. Describe a time when you found yourself worrying about how long your feelings of depersonalization might go on. How did worrying affect your experience?

3. We are pretty good at relieving discomfort that has a physical origin. Has thinking about *physical* pain led you to new strategies for treating any physical complaint (such as a cold, a chipped tooth, a headache, and so on)? Were your efforts successful?

4. Has thinking about psychological pain led to relief or more pain? How successful have you been in your efforts to solve the problem of depersonalization?

EXERCISE: Experiencing Self-Focus

The purpose of this exercise is to see how thinking a lot about your suffering leads to more suffering and more self-focus. Read through the following exercise carefully before completing it; try to remember the instructions as you go along. If you have trouble remembering the instructions, you might want to slowly read them into an audio recorder so you can play them back later.

Close your eyes and concentrate on the sensation of breathing; just bring awareness to the way it feels to take air into your abdomen. Notice how automatically you normally breathe. For a few moments, just acknowledge the rhythm of this bodily function.

1. Bring your awareness to your thoughts. Notice what your mind brings up. With present-moment awareness, just try to observe your thought process, how tangential your thoughts can be, and how readily they flock to negative or distressing topics.

2. Take note of how depersonalized you feel right now. How in touch with your sensations are you right now? How capable of human emotion do you feel right now? How easily are you able

to concentrate on this activity? To what extent do you feel that you're inside your own body right now? Just take note of this.

3. Now concentrate on a few discrete thoughts and just acknowledge how your mind reacts to each statement. Try to observe how your feelings change as certain topics are brought to your immediate awareness; just observe your internal reactions, directly.

Think: *I'll never be able to have a meaningful relationship.*

How does your mind respond to this thought? Does it agree or disagree? Did it get carried away with this idea? Do you notice any change in your mood while thinking this thought? Just notice any changes that occur in your mood.

Think: *I'll always feel this sense of estrangement from myself.*

Again, acknowledge how your mind "talks back" to this thought. How does this thought affect your mood? Do you feel more hopeless? Just notice how thinking this thought colors your sensations and feelings.

Think: *Doctors will never be able to help me. I'm all on my own. Nobody without this condition knows how bad this feels.*

Just be aware of whether your mind has a reaction to this thought. Take note of what thoughts come up in response. Do these ideas resonate with you? Again, take notice of your mood. Does meditating on these thoughts affect how you feel?

Think: *How can I possibly go on with this sense of unreality?*

Acknowledge your thoughts and any mood changes you have.

4. Again, bring your attention to how depersonalized you feel right now. Have your feelings of depersonalization changed at all since the exercise began? Notice any overall changes in your emotions, sensations, and thoughts. Just take stock of your overall internal experience.

When you are ready, bring your attention back to the external environment and open your eyes.

How did focusing on negative thoughts affect your mood? How did focusing on the sentiments that often go along with chronic depersonalization affect your feelings of detachment? Many people who participate in this exercise notice that focusing on a thought about DPD and its corresponding acknowledgment of how "terrible" this is heightens their discomfort. This exercise highlights the idea that language has an immense capacity to influence feelings and that always using our feelings to guide our behavior can become a very dangerous default state. For example, if someone believes she will never be able to have a meaningful relationship, if she really buys into this thought and becomes despondent as a result, it's easy to see how she may totally stop trying to find companionship if she allows those feelings of despondence to dictate her behavior. In this book, we'll offer strategies to help you let go of your distressing thoughts and live your life the way you want to.

Acceptance: The Alternative to Problem Solving

Notice that self-focus, rumination, and obsession about depersonalization often lead to problem-solving thoughts: *What can I do to get rid of this feeling? How am I going to live if I have to go on this way? How can I feel better?* When it comes to depersonalization, a problem-solving orientation may work against you. Efforts to get rid of unpleasant thoughts, emotions, and sensations may just make the experiences all the more intolerable. So, what *can* you do? The alternative is being willing to experience the feeling, to stop the war with negative thinking, and to give your discomfort some room to be there as you work toward living the life you want. In chapters 5, 6, and 7, we'll address mindfulness and acceptance as an alternative to changing your thoughts and feelings, in order to give you a wider range of strategies and a greater sense of peace. Mindfulness and acceptance might sound difficult, but throughout the book, we'll teach you practical strategies that you can incorporate into your everyday life.

Just because problem-solving your way out of depersonalization doesn't work, this doesn't mean that your life has to continue in the direction of depersonalization or that you'll never be able to enjoy the things you once enjoyed. On the contrary, what we are suggesting is that worrying and trying to solve an emotional struggle by making the feelings go away is counterproductive and, in fact, may just prolong your agony. Therefore, our focus will be on improving how you function, rather than exclusively on improving how you feel.

SUMMARY

Though it's human nature for us to try to beat psychological discomfort by getting rid of it, thinking about discomfort may only make the discomfort more real to us. While thinking about our problems may help us to solve problems in the external realm, it only leads to added discomfort in the internal world. Depersonalization may get worse when you try to get rid of it. As you learned from the exercises in this chapter, thinking about your feelings of depersonalization may actually serve to heighten them.

Depersonalization may also get worse when you try to avoid its accompanying feelings of discomfort. When we avoid unpleasant feelings, we also tend to avoid important life areas. Those areas of life we tend to value the most are those in which we suffer the most. Therefore, when you struggle with depersonalization, you may develop an inflexible routine to try limiting your discomfort, but doing so also limits your richness and diversity of experience. As we proceed, we'll discuss ways you can ensure that you don't neglect valued life areas *while* you're experiencing feelings of depersonalization.

3

Why Depersonalization
Disorder Develops

You are probably wondering how and why you ended up with DPD. Where did it come from? Human behavior is influenced by a tremendously vast pool of variables, including environmental, cultural, and biological aspects. In this chapter, we'll explore what might have led to your developing DPD.

The Impact of Trauma

We find that many people with DPD have experienced some form of trauma in the past. What is traumatic for one person may not be so for another, but many people with DPD describe the past as filled with chaos and difficulties with family members—to such an extent they felt they had to escape. They somehow managed to do what they had to do to survive. Sometimes, the trauma is complex and cumulative, and other times, it may be just one big incident. Some of the types of traumas we have encountered are child abuse (physical, sexual, or emotional), rape, an alcoholic or gambling parent, and constant parental conflict with yelling and screaming.

In the case of child abuse, the situation often lasts for many years. Researchers who study victims of such horrors found that there was a high incidence of dissociative symptoms in these populations, especially when the victim was abused as a child, whether sexually, physically, or through neglect (Svedin, Nilsson, and Lindell 2004). However, physical abuse is the type most often associated with dissociation.

In effect, dissociation works as a defense that separates the pain from your conscious mind, thereby helping you to maintain composure. Think about it: under normal circumstances, if someone hit you in the face, you might be shocked or get very angry; your body would go into fight-or-flight mode, making you alert and anxious. Now imagine that someone hits you in the face every five minutes for the rest of the year. Eventually your body will stop responding to the shock of the impact so that you become acclimated to these terrible circumstances; your mind and body must adjust. It's only natural. Depersonalization works similarly in some people: when you are faced with tremendous or enduring discomfort, your mind and body basically stop paying attention, leaving you in a numb state, numb to the pain, of course, but simultaneously numb to everything else. Researchers generally agree that victimization and maltreatment in childhood can indeed be the source of dissociative symptoms and that, while these symptoms are sometimes temporary, they interfere with normal psychological development in adulthood.

Abuse is not the only circumstance under which depersonalization develops; other environmental factors also play a part. Children who were exposed to community violence (Horowitz, Weine, and Jekel 1995), large-scale accidents (Yule, Udwin, and Murdoch 1990), or war (Kinzie et al. 1986) were more likely to exhibit psychiatric symptoms. Past research shows that people who are raised among poverty are more likely to experience dissociative disorders (Altman 1995). You may be wondering how this relates to you if you neither were raised in poverty nor witnessed torture or terrorism. However, you may have been a victim of a theft or home invasion, a witness of a shoot-out, a victim of bullying as a child, or disturbed by neglectful or volatile parenting. So read on because, although some of the work that has been done may not sound as if it relates to you directly, it may apply indirectly.

In a psychopathology study (Ilechukwu 2007) conducted in a Nigerian hospital, researchers discovered that 25 percent of the patients there related having dissociative symptoms. Many Nigerian children are sent off to live with nonrelatives at a very early age to work to earn money for their families and gain access to education. However, enduring both physical and sexual abuse is another price they very commonly have to pay. In cases where the child remains in this type of situation, it seems that dissociative symptoms allow the child to escape from the abusive experiences, at least in mind.

You don't have to experience a trauma directly to develop DPD. Perhaps at some point or another, someone in your family experienced a trauma. Research shows that even if you are a bystander to trauma, you, too, can develop the same sort of reaction (Seligman and Kirmayer 2008). For example, if a child who resulted from a rape is made aware of her beginnings, this legacy might cause significant emotional trauma for her while growing up, and may contribute negatively to her development. When researchers examine the causes of dissociative disorders, context is a crucial factor to consider (ibid.). If an event seems significant to your social environment, peers, or family, you are likely to consider it significant too.

Trauma from Cultural Assimilation

Disruption of cultural identity could also become a source of trauma. Emigration to a completely different culture or exposure to sociohistorical events (such as tyranny or terrorism) may cause intense feelings of fear or shame, resulting in trauma (Bodnar 2004). For example, if a family moves to a contrasting culture, the parents may stumble in their child rearing until they relearn how to raise their children in the midst of the new culture. Were your parents immigrants who struggled to find their way in American culture, and did you feel traumatized when you had friends over?

Multicultural people may consequently struggle to identify securely with social roles. For example, researcher Etty Cohen (2007) conveys a story about a study participant in the Israeli army who experienced a great disturbance when he felt sympathy for Palestinian women begging for their imprisoned husbands' release, even though they were technically the "enemy." The person dissociated to maintain personal continuity and integrity of his sense of self (Bromberg 1996), because this sort of paradox forces the mind to employ defensive strategies to conceptualize both views simultaneously: "Culturally, they are the enemy and are to be hated" and "Humanely, they are fellows begging for mercy, and deserve sympathy." In essence, dissociation is an adaptive means of psychological survival, a battle for consistency in the face of inconsistency (Pizer 1998).

Trauma from Disruptive Family Relations

Okay, so maybe you're asking, "Who doesn't come from some sort of dysfunctional family?" Well, there *are* some healthy families, but setting that aside for the moment, what matters is how we cope with our disruptive family relations. Let me give you an example of a man who described his family as "one from hell." He remembers that as a child, he didn't know much for certain, but he did know he couldn't tolerate all that yelling and screaming going on. His mother was an alcoholic and his father was absent a lot but emotionally abusive when at home. The two of them fought every night until the wee hours of the morning, and the only way the boy and his brother could cope was to hide in their rooms, shut the door, and drift into fantasyland. The only emotion expressed in the family was anger, through yelling.

Another person, who had chronic DPD for years but didn't know it except for the numbness she experienced, described her family as "the fire department." They were always trying to extinguish the heated chaos of her younger sister, who was off creating one problem after another that needed immediate attention. Sometimes the issues were very trivial, but the reactions of her sister and, subsequently, her parents, who were always trying to calm the sister down, were extreme. Her parents would get exhausted and angry, eventually giving up for the moment, only to return to chaotic, uncontrollable responses later. Her father would sometimes get angry at her mother, who was helpless (but trying), and thus he would retreat into his bedroom for days on end. Her parents were really never there for her; it was as if she didn't exist. She remembers coping all right as a younger child, periodically disappearing into her own world and reemerging. Eventually, in her teens, her depersonalization set in for a long time.

As you can see, what's most critical is your perception of your family situation and how you deal with it, rather than what's actually happening. This is true for all problems in life.

Cultural Factors That Contribute to Depersonalization

In certain cultures, depersonalization or other dissociative symptoms may come about as a means to maintain socially acceptable behavior. For example, in the Balinese culture, self-preservation is associated with stoicism, and emotional pain is swept aside to constantly present a facade of smoothness and strength to others (Wikan 1990). Members of other cultures avoid strong emotions because they are thought to correlate with bad health (Wellenkamp 2002). In some parts of Turkey, it's not acceptable to express emotions such as depression or anxiety, so people may develop hypochondriacal symptoms, dissociate, or both to avoid experiencing unacceptable negative emotions. Therefore, in cultures where emotional expression is discouraged, dissociation may be a preferable alternative if you are struggling with intense unpleasant emotions.

In certain cultures, dissociative experiences may also take place in socially sanctioned rituals and religious healing practices. However, this kind of dissociation may be desirable in these cultures rather than a sign of psychopathology. In less extreme forms, we all enter into a dissociative state at times, when we become totally unaware of our environment. We may be unaware of most of the external environment and become completely and narrowly focused on a single object, such as a book or the television, or an activity, such as playing a sport or simply daydreaming. This widely accepted form of dissociation is not only entered into voluntarily at times but also socially accepted and often reinforced (Butler and Palesh 2004). Dissociation of this type is seen as a useful technique (Seligman and Kirmayer 2008).

The Effect of Substance Abuse

You may have been one of the many who developed your first depersonalization experience after smoking pot. We have all heard of the "munchies" and the paranoia that can ensue after smoking, but who ever heard of remaining dissociated for days, weeks, months, or even years afterward? Yes, you can have a perceptual change after smoking pot, but that goes away the next day or in a few hours, right? Well, maybe not.

When Emily smoked marijuana with some friends at age fourteen, it was a bad experience from the beginning. With the onset of the psychoactive effects, she immediately became extremely panicked. She felt as though she had no control over her body, that she was slipping away. Occasionally she felt she was coming to, but only to get completely "fogged over" again. The initial sensations dissipated over time, but the overall feeling of dissociation did not. She would go to sleep expecting to feel normal in the morning but, when morning came, would feel no different. She kept drinking coffee, eating, and trying to sleep it off, anything to change her frame of mind, but once depersonalization came on, it never left her.

How can you know whether you would have the same reaction to smoking pot? Actually, there's no way to predict this. You might be one of the lucky ones for whom it happens once and then disappears. If that's the case, then it might be best not to smoke again, in case you're not so lucky next time. Apparently, if you have a permanent reaction, such as Emily had, your body chemistry doesn't jibe well with the stuff. Marijuana can trigger panic attacks, dissociative states, or some combination of the two; or it can have no psychologically remarkable effect at all (Simeon 2004). Some people note that pot makes them more introverted and more aware of perceptual changes, which echoes depersonalization. Things seem to be at a distance, their ability to respond to questions slows down, they don't think clearly, and their hands and body seem estranged. All those sensations may be enjoyable for a brief time, but if you are depersonalized, it's an awful experience, one that may not go away. Although pot is the most common trigger, it could be any other drug. Other hallucinogens may also cause this reaction, such as PCP, DXM, or ketamine (also known as "Special K") (ibid.).

Neurobiology of Depersonalization

Because your brain is the control center of your body, it controls your feelings, movement, and perceptions. Naturally, you might wonder about the connection between this biological computer and the dissociative symptoms you experience. While some of the data on the neurobiology of DPD remains inconsistent and inconclusive, in this section we'll discuss recent findings to give you an idea of where the research is taking us.

Researchers Mauricio Sierra and German E. Berrios (2001) compared historical reports of dissociation disorder with those of study participants in 2001. Their results showed consistency of clinical manifestations (reported symptoms and so on) over time. In other words, despite the vast changes that have occurred in culture and society throughout history, symptoms of DPD are relatively constant. So it makes sense to say that there's some unchanging, innate biology involved in the disorder.

It's necessary for you to get a basic explanation of brain anatomy and function to fully understand the nature of your symptoms. For your convenience, we have included a diagram of the brain that clearly labels the parts to which we'll refer.

One way to look at the nervous system relates to aroused versus resting neural reactions, both known as *autonomic reactions*. The *parasympathetic* (resting) and *sympathetic* (aroused or anxious) systems comprise autonomic functioning. If you are presented with a life-threatening situation (for example, a man with a gun is chasing you down a dark alley), your sympathetic system will be activated. Your eyes will dilate so that you are more alert to details in the darkness. Your heart and breathing rate will become more rapid to more effectively supply your organs with oxygen (so you can move more quickly and have a better chance of getting to safety). Your kidneys will release adrenaline, also in an effort to speed up your escape. In effect, your body will be sympathetic to your current need to flee from a predator in the quickest and most effective way possible.

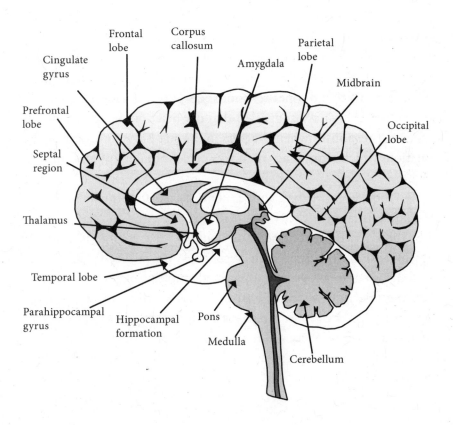

Other processes, like digestion, sexual arousal, pupil constriction, and relaxation of the heart and breathing rate, are considered resting or relaxing activities and are unnecessary at very crucial, stressful moments. These functions are hindered when the sympathetic nervous system is activated because they are the job of the parasympathetic system. Basically, the sympathetic system is active when you need to be alert, and the parasympathetic system is active when arousal is not necessary. As you may have guessed, the sympathetic and parasympathetic nervous systems are contradictory, and only one can function at a time.

In people with anxiety disorders, the sympathetic system is overactive. Interestingly, many people who have DPD also have significant amounts of anxiety or, indeed, an anxiety disorder (Baker et al. 2003). As we discussed before, DPD can often occur as a result of some horrific trauma, such as childhood sexual or physical abuse. With this in mind, it seems that DPD might represent a mechanism by which autonomic emotional responses are inhibited in the face of underlying anxiety. In other words, depersonalization might diminish emotional reactions, despite enduring discomfort. Some researchers have suggested that dissociation occurs to inhibit emotional responses when the person doesn't have control over the situation, which rings true when we speak about abuse and the like (ibid.).

Further, when people with DPD undergo functional magnetic resonance imaging (fMRI, an MRI machine that actually shows brain activity in real time) and look at distressing or disgusting images, their sympathetic responses are reduced (Phillips et al. 2001). People with DPD also rated unpleasant pictures as less arousing (Sierra et al. 2002) and were less sensitive to detection of angry facial expressions. Anger communicates a great threat and usually induces anxiety, so it fits that people with DPD have an inhibited response to pictures showing such a provocative emotion (Montagne et al. 2007).

Your brain has a fascinating method of chemical communication: it uses *neurotransmitters,* which are chemicals that carry specific messages. Examples of neurotransmitters include serotonin, dopamine, and endorphins. Greater levels of norepinephrine (a neurotransmitter that's greatly involved in anxiety) are found in people with *less severe* DPD than severe DPD. In other words, severe DPD causes a suppression of the neurotransmitters associated with anxiety (Simeon et al. 2003a). This finding supports the idea that dissociation is an inhibitory mechanism for autonomic emotional responses.

Although the research is incomplete, three types of neurotransmitter systems seem to be involved in dissociation:

Diminished NMDA-Related Neurotransmission. NMDA (N-methyl D-aspartate) can be found in the cortex (the outer section of your brain), the hippocampus (involved in memory), and the amygdala (which plays a lead role in prominent emotions such as fear and anger), and is believed to be involved in intensity of long-term memory. The drugs ketamine ("Special K") (Curran and Morgan 2000) and marijuana (Feigenbaum et al. 1989), both of which block NMDA-related activity in the brain, are known to cause profound dissociative states.

Increased Serotonin Activity. Serotonin is a multipurpose neurotransmitter that's involved in sleep, depression, and memory, among other psychological experiences. Increased serotonin activity can cause dissociative symptoms (Simeon et al. 1995). Further, drugs that increase serotonin activity (such as lysergide, or LSD) induce depersonalization (Simeon et al. 2003b).

Increased Opioid Activity. When under great duress, the body protects itself from pain with natural opioids (endorphins). Drugs that block opioid activity (such as naloxone, which is used to treat those with chronic depersonalization) reduce dissociative symptoms (Nuller et al. 2001).

Neuroanatomy of Depersonalization

Let's switch gears from neurochemistry to neuroanatomy. Have you ever seen those cartoons of a compartmentalized brain, with television, sex, your career, playing a musical instrument, and so on separated in little cubicles? While the details of those cartoons are usually vastly inaccurate, the general idea behind them *is* true: different parts of your brain serve different functions. Some functions require only one part of your brain to work, independently, while many others require more than one part to work in conjunction or in sequence.

While research on the neurobiology of depersonalization disorder is scant, it's rather convincing.

When shown a series of aversive scenes that would normally produce a reaction of disgust (cockroaches lined up according to size), study participants with DPD rated them as less emotive than did the control group (Phillips and Sierra 2003). Further, the participants with DPD showed reduced activity in the insula, which is the part of your brain that's active when you feel disgusted, and increased activity in the ventrolateral prefrontal cortex which has been implicated in appraisal of emotionally meaningful material and memories. Other studies have used a positron emission tomography (PET) scan, which measures blood, oxygen, and glucose flow in the brain. The following findings are a bit technical, but bear with us:

- The more severe the depersonalization symptoms were (during marijuana use), the greater the blood flow in the right frontal and anterior cingulate cortexes (which contribute to a vast array of autonomic functions, including emotion) (Mathew et al. 1999).

- Decreased blood flow was observed in the amygdala, hippocampus, and basal ganglia (involved in feeling and thinking) (Simeon 2004).

- Decreased blood flow was also observed in the thalamus (which relays relevant information to the parts of your brain that regulate sensation and arousal) (ibid.).

Basically, these findings might suggest that certain parts of the brain aren't working together properly. The overactivity of the prefrontal cortex may inhibit activity of the *limbic system* (the neurological emotion center, including the amygdala and the hippocampus). This, as the researchers suggested, leads to hypoemotionality or, as many people with DPD describe it, emotional numbness or deadness (Simeon and Abugel 2006).

A study by D. Simeon and colleagues (2000) yielded somewhat different, but not contradictory, results. Study participants with DPD had decreased metabolic activity in the right temporal lobe and significantly higher metabolic activity was observed in the parietal lobe and the left occipital lobe. The temporal, parietal, and occipital lobes are generally associated with auditory, somatosensory (touch), and visual senses, respectively. While this all might be a bit technical for our purposes, the overall idea is that the integration of your emotions and your sensations may be abnormal from a neurological standpoint. This could explain why you feel "disconnected" or "distant" from your own body and the environment. As we experience it, consciousness is the integration of various cortical areas (Krystal et al. 1998), so it makes perfect sense that the *disruption* of that consciousness involves abnormalities in several cortical regions (or a disruption of communication among these areas).

This is not the first time someone has taken a "sensory" approach to DPD. Neurologist Wilder G. Penfield postulated the "temporal lobe hypothesis" of depersonalization in 1950 (Penfield and Rasmussen 1950). He was able to induce dissociation in people by stimulating parts of their temporal lobes. In doing so, he believed that he interrupted the mechanism that assimilates memories of sensory experiences. For example, my hand has always been connected to my wrist, and in my memory, I've always used my hands to touch, feel, and grasp. I have always known that I can move my hands around if I want to. Penfield would say that stimulating parts of my temporal lobe might interfere with the association between my hand and body; for example, my hand would no longer feel as if it belonged to my body. His hypothesis was later supported by other research, which found depersonalization to be a common symptom among people with temporal lobe epilepsy (Harper and Roth 1962).

SUMMARY

Depersonalization disorder may be triggered by psychological, biological, chemical, or environmental events. In short, DPD may come about as a result of:

- Trauma from traumatic events, including abuse, neglect, sociohistorical events, extreme stress, or trauma associated with another psychological condition (for example, anxiety present during OCD symptomatic periods)

- Use of drugs such as marijuana, ketamine ("Special K"), or other hallucinogens, which may trigger a DPD episode

- Neurochemical or neuroanatomical abnormalities in the form of transmission of certain neurochemicals that may affect the experience of depersonalization, and communication among certain areas of the brain that may also interfere with sensory integration, contributing to DPD

4

Understanding Conditions Related to Depersonalization Disorder

Depersonalization is a symptom that's associated with many disorders. It's also an adaptive way of dealing with difficult emotions many of us have experienced at one time or another, as we discussed in chapter 3. This chapter explores how this adaptive process may go awry and become dysfunctional. We'll also examine how dysfunctional depersonalization may be seen in a variety of psychological conditions.

The Two Types of Depersonalization

Two types of depersonalization exist: chronic (or primary) and episodic (or secondary). As discussed in the preceding chapter, depersonalization may refer to a disorder, but it may also describe a symptom. The former is primary DPD (it generally sticks around for a long time and is, in and of itself, a psychologically destructive force); the latter is episodic (shorter in duration and more adaptive, and it usually comes and goes with extreme psychological stress). We'll discuss episodic depersonalization first.

Episodic Depersonalization

Episodic (secondary) depersonalization may often seem to be chronic, even though it goes away after a while. When you experience the emotional numbness and altered sense of self of depersonalization, you may be led to ask, "Will this ever go away?" It may seem as if you'll never return to reality as you knew it. However, episodic depersonalization *will* go away, although it's hard to predict when. It could go away in a day, a month, or, in some cases, several months. Yet, unlike chronic depersonalization, it's not there to stay for a long time.

From an evolutionary perspective, episodic depersonalization is quite reasonable: if we are in a situation that's relentlessly emotionally depleting or extremely traumatic, it benefits us to adopt a robot-like sense of awareness. Think for a moment why that may be. Did you ever notice that when you are extremely emotional, you don't reason well? When you experience episodic depersonalization, you may feel a sense of unreality or transcendence, a subjective sense of being outside of yourself, or a feeling that you aren't responsible for your actions. In a sense, you are able to act *without* emotional involvement, which can sometimes be a good thing. However, this sensation may pass as soon as the extreme emotions have passed. Depersonalization of this variety may be a healthy and natural tendency within our emotional repertoire; when faced with extreme emotional discomfort, the mind will sometimes make an effort to put the body on autopilot to avoid emotionally directed, impulsive decision making that might do more harm than good. However, this important emotional response has the potential to go awry in some people.

Chronic Depersonalization

Let's look at what the mind does when we sense danger. When the mind determines that the body is somehow threatened, it sends out a distress signal notifying us that we are in danger and that we should do something quickly. This is the fight-or-flight response we often hear about. You get ready to either attack or run away. For example, while driving, if we sense that an accident is about to occur, we immediately swerve the car away or hit the brakes. Obviously, this is a quick response, directed toward a momentary threat. However, if the source of the threat represents a long-standing or unavoidable danger, the distress signal is sent out over and over again, fruitlessly. After a period of prolonged distress, the mind may eventually try to inhibit the emotional reaction if repeated acknowledgment of discomfort doesn't result in relief. For example, if as a child you endured extreme neglect and did everything at the time to get the care you needed without success, eventually your discomfort would no longer give you any new information. As a result, your mind may inhibit the emotional reaction, because it's not doing you any good. We have seen many people who described their childhood as full of chaos, where their parents were unable to take care of their needs. As kids they knew something was wrong but didn't know what it was. They hid in their rooms a lot of the time or dreamed of having different parents. In some of these cases, the parents were alcoholics or had gambling problems, and in others, they were too busy arguing to notice their children, to the extent that fighting, yelling, and screaming were the norm. This type of early childhood may contribute to the development of chronic (or primary) depersonalization. Ironically, the adaptive depersonalization response becomes the problem itself, and the mind and body are unable to return to a pattern of typical awareness of emotional and perceptual information. What results is a state of alienation from your experiences, which is characterized by obsessive preoccupation with psychological discomfort and a sense of altered reality.

Chronic depersonalization may be thought of as a sort of cancer of adaptive functioning; it's an overgrowth of a healthy and protective response to trauma and discomfort. As discussed in the previous chapter, trauma is abrupt or prolonged exposure to something that elicits an extreme emotional reaction, including the death of a loved one, continued emotional abuse, or negligent parenting. Anything that causes extreme discomfort may bring about an experience of depersonalization. If this experience doesn't resolve, it may become the primary source of your discomfort. However, it's important to note that chronic depersonalization may develop randomly, without any identifiable trigger, or it may have a rapid onset following a brief exposure to a distressing event or incident of drug use. As mentioned in the previous chapter, some people say they feel depersonalized after using marijuana, others after experiencing severe anxiety or depression. Sometimes it's hard to identify any precipitating event. Also, it's not uncommon for people who smoked marijuana several times in the past without incident to, all of a sudden, find that continued smoking of marijuana has led them to a chronic state of depersonalization. So it's important to understand that a direct relationship between precipitating events and chronic depersonalization is currently unclear. However, investigations have repeatedly acknowledged that depersonalization is commonly observed in people who have endured trauma, whether acute or prolonged.

The three people with DPD presented earlier in the book allude to various precipitants of the disorder. Emily said that chronic DPD developed after marijuana use; John attributed the onset of DPD to playing football, though he never sustained any significant injuries; and Susan suddenly developed a pattern of isolation and depersonalization for no specific reason. Another person we worked with, Danny, associated feelings of depersonalization with a period when he endured consistent verbal abuse from his mother. The experiences of these people illustrate that while DPD symptoms tend to arise in response to extreme discomfort, direct cause is not always clear.

Diagnosis of DPD

With these considerations in mind, it's also important to think about depersonalization in the context of individual functioning. As with all psychological disturbances, symptoms of depersonalization disorder exist on a continuum. The severity of symptoms and the degree to which they interfere with daily functioning determine whether symptoms of depersonalization warrant a diagnosis of depersonalization disorder. In other words, if you find that depersonalization interferes with your functioning or if you are incredibly uncomfortable due to depersonalization symptoms, you may have DPD. Typically, psychological functioning is evaluated in several ways, including professional, social, and academic functioning, as well as many other areas. For example, failing four out of five classes in a semester would demonstrate difficulty maintaining academic functioning, being reprimanded by your boss for neglecting professional responsibilities may indicate that your work functioning is in jeopardy, and frequent fighting with your spouse would indicate difficulty with social functioning. The four stories we've introduced indicate impairment in all of these areas. All four people expressed having difficulty in romantic relationships due to feelings of depersonalization. While three out of the four people described were able to continue functioning at work, most of them related that they were able to cope only as a "robot." You may find yourself disinterested in intimacy and social contacts because you become more aware of your inability to relate during interactions, which compounds distress. You may find it difficult to focus and concentrate, so you avoid mentally strenuous activities, thereby interfering with professional and academic performance. Your experiences with depersonalization, the resulting personal and professional consequences, and the degree to which they interfere with comfort and functioning determine whether a diagnosis of DPD (or primary depersonalization) is warranted.

Depersonalization and Other Psychological Conditions

As explained earlier, depersonalization is a symptom that may be present in many disorders other than chronic (primary) depersonalization (DPD). Next, we present a few related conditions and how they relate to experiences of depersonalization. You may find that you can identify with some of these conditions in addition to depersonalization, but keep in mind that only a trained and knowledgeable mental health professional can make a diagnosis. The following disorders may mimic depersonalization at times.

Panic Disorder

A panic attack occurs when a person experiences anxiety so strongly that she feels she may lose control. Symptoms of a panic attack include racing heartbeat, tingling in the extremities, shortness of breath, dizziness, change in blood pressure or faintness, and a sense of impending death, among other symptoms. Panic and depersonalization share many commonalities. Panic arises when someone is faced with circumstances that elicit extreme discomfort, and the same may be said for depersonalization. Like people with DPD, panic-disordered people usually respond with physical symptoms that make them uncomfortable and lead to panic under a variety of circumstances, whether or not it's warranted. As is true with depersonalization, a panic attack may arise regardless of whether legitimate danger exists. In this way, both panic disorder and depersonalization disorder may be likened to a car alarm, rightfully going off when a person tries to break in, but also erroneously going off when a strong wind hits it.

Emily, one of the people with DPD introduced in chapter 1, described initial symptoms of panic disorder. She became preoccupied by the fear of losing control, which is pretty common among people with panic disorder. Susan described something similar: experiencing depersonalization in social settings. She, too, mentioned a feeling of losing control, which is also common for people with DPD:

When I'm around a group of people, it's like my brain checks out. I'm no longer there but somewhere slightly outside myself. I'm able to watch my reactions and to understand the feelings that should be there, but I suddenly feel that I don't have control over what I do. It's as if I've made a prior arrangement with my body about what it will do, as if my reactions are socially acceptable but aren't immediately coming from me. Feeling like you're not the one in control makes you feel that you're totally out of control, even if everything looks calm from the exterior.

Depersonalization can occur with or without extreme anxiety, and panic may be present with or without a feeling of being outside yourself, but many people describe a significant overlap in these experiences.

Depersonalization and panic are both symptoms of disorders, but aren't necessarily inherently pathological. Depersonalization is an emotional reaction that initially protects the person experiencing it, and panic alerts us to sources of danger. Our ancestors needed to react quickly and with a fight-or-flight reaction; they needed to be hypervigilant to avoid danger. From an evolutionary perspective, if something helps us avoid death, it will likely get passed on to the next generation, even if it becomes excessive and causes distress. Again, the same may be said for depersonalization; it's an initially adaptive reaction that can cause its own host of problems when it's provoked in inappropriate and unnecessary situations. In fact, DPD and panic disorder frequently co-occur. Researchers found that 73 percent of study participants with DPD experienced panic attacks (Baker et al. 2003). Depersonalization episodes occur sometimes during and sometimes immediately following panic attacks, suggesting that panic and depersonalization responses are related. Panic disorder is more severe when accompanied by depersonalization, with higher rates of agoraphobia (fear of public places) and earlier age of onset (Cassano et al. 1989). Some theorists believe that depersonalization may represent an extension of an extreme anxiety reaction (that is, panic may lead to depersonalization in certain people). However, it's an oversimplification to say that depersonalization is merely a reaction to anxiety, because DPD is observed with and without anxiety disorders.

Interoceptive cue exposure, which is exposure to the physiological symptoms of anxiety arousal, is a therapeutic approach used by behavioral therapists to treat panic disorder. Because many symptoms of depersonalization overlap with symptoms of panic, interoceptive cue exposure may be useful in treating DPD. We'll present techniques for exposing yourself to feared internal sensations in chapter 8. Also, acceptance strategies, which will be introduced in chapters 5, 6, and 7, will provide you with techniques for fostering willingness to experience the discomfort associated with depersonalization.

Post-Traumatic Stress Disorder

Certain people who are exposed to extreme trauma over short- or long-term intervals experience post-traumatic stress disorder

(PTSD). The victim of a rape may develop PTSD; likewise, a soldier exposed to graphic combat situations may also develop it. Post-traumatic reaction generally involves flashbacks related to the imagery of the traumatic event, avoidance of situations that may remind the person of the traumatic event, and emotional withdrawal related to PTSD distress. Efforts to avoid distressing emotions and scenarios are observed in both PTSD and DPD. Furthermore, as elaborated previously, depersonalization is a common reaction to extreme emotional discomfort, so depersonalization and post-traumatic reactions are commonly observed in the same survivors of traumatic incidents. In fact, diagnostic criteria for PTSD in the *DSM-IV-TR* indicate that dissociation is common. For example, people with PTSD may experience dissociation when recalling traumatic events, or they may describe feelings of detachment or estrangement from others, or difficulty concentrating.

While the number of people with DPD who also meet criteria for PTSD is relatively low (approximately 5 percent), the experience of trauma is very common (Simeon and Abugel 2006). Danny, one of the people with DPD previously mentioned, related that enduring verbal abuse from his mother precipitated his feelings of depersonalization. This is a common feature among people with chronic DPD. Extreme emotional experiences may also constitute mild trauma, especially if you have a heightened sensitivity to distress. For example, some studies have shown that people may tell of having depersonalization during and following a period of extreme psychological discomfort (like a major depressive episode, for example). Long-standing, daily stress or overwork may also evoke or exacerbate DPD. Theoretically, the more severe a traumatic incident is, the less exposure is needed to elicit a dissociative reaction. For example, someone must endure extreme work stress for a long time for it to lead to a dissociative reaction, while one instance of sexual abuse may be enough to cause dissociation. It's also important to note that the interplay of many factors seems to contribute to the onset of dissociation or depersonalization. For example, the age at which the person experiences the trauma and the person's sensitivity to distress may affect whether or not the person experiences depersonalization.

Obsessive-Compulsive Disorder

Many people with OCD relate qualities of depersonalization as well. One study found that people with OCD, especially with checking and ordering or arranging behaviors, also met criteria for depersonalization disorder (Rufer et al. 2006), and approximately one-third of people with dissociative identity disorder exhibited obsessive-compulsive symptoms (Kluft 1993). A prominent symptom of OCD involves obsessive preoccupation with philosophical issues. Philosophical obsession is characterized by persistent, intrusive focus on the meaning of existence, theological issues, or personal purpose. People with obsessive philosophical thoughts may muse over their own mortality, often communicating that they have inner turmoil related to some sort of existential dilemma. Content of philosophical obsessions is frequently very negative (for example, "What's the purpose of living?" "Why do we go on if we are simply going to die?" and so on), and thoughts reoccur in a relentless, nagging manner. This symptom is also commonly found among people with DPD (that is, intellectual focus on distressing topics related to philosophy and existence). You may have noticed obsessive thoughts about your symptoms of depersonalization, but you may also have obsessions about greater philosophical matters (for example, pondering the existence of the human soul, whether you lack a "self," whether you can thrive with a permanent sense of personal and spiritual emptiness, and the like).

Susan, a person with DPD introduced in chapter 2, had philosophical obsessions, such as uncertainty about the autonomy of her actions and the purpose of living. Doubting of autonomy is directly reminiscent of OCD, which is often referred to as the "doubting disease." Essentially, OCD causes people to doubt their observations, even though their observational ability and critical thinking are intact. A sense of being unable to trust or tap into feelings is clearly very common in DPD as well. It's easy to see the overlap between philosophical obsessions and depersonalization; you don't have to probe too deeply into ancient and modern philosophy to see that the mind-body connection has plagued mankind for all of recorded history.

Obsessive thinking in general may be observed among people with DPD. Have you found that you relentlessly focus on symptoms related to your discomfort, on your inability to tap into those feelings, and on how miserable it would be to live this way indefinitely? People with chronic DPD believe that their symptoms will never improve. Furthermore, obsessive focus on physiological precipitants of depersonalization resembles hypochondriasis (obsessive-compulsive monitoring for symptoms of a serious illness). If you are like most of the people we know with DPD, you spend countless hours researching and self-monitoring to determine whether depersonalization has some neurological or physiological basis. You may have been evaluated for a variety of health issues, including Lyme disease, brain tumors, mercury poisoning, Alzheimer's disease, and other forms of dementia. Almost every person with DPD we see in therapy tells of having received PET scans, CT scans, MRIs, and the like in an effort to find some physical explanation for depersonalization symptoms. Preoccupation with health is extremely common among people with DPD, OCD, and hypochondriasis. However, it's important to note that obsessive focus on DPD symptoms is related to seeking an explanation for discomfort rather than fear of terminal illness.

Depersonalization disorder is considered an obsessive-compulsive spectrum disorder due to the relentlessness of obsessive thinking, the reciprocally reinforcing nature of symptoms, and the preoccupation with those symptoms. In other words, people with both DPD and OCD will become preoccupied with evidence of symptoms and then focus on these symptoms; any distress will then be compounded by hypervigilance for discomfort, thereby exacerbating symptoms and obsessive thinking about them. In short, both disorders are more or less self-sustaining vicious cycles that frequently spiral out of control. For example, at the onset of deper-sonalization, it may suddenly occur to you that you're not experi-encing reality as you used to. Maybe this involves being unable to tap into feelings of love. Once the permanence of this state becomes a tragic realization, you might sit and just observe internal experi-ences, searching for feelings of love. Then possibly, during this pursuit, you notice how fleeting your feelings are and how diffi-cult it is to will yourself to tap into a feeling. Acknowledgment of the elusiveness of your feelings might feel a bit like loss of control, which may be very distressing to you because you already feel as if you can't trust your experiences. Sensations of loss of control then become something to fear, and any internal sensation that may be interpreted as loss of control will become obsessively preoccupying. You may interpret sensations that have nothing to do with DPD as such, making it harder and harder for you to just get out of your own head. This concept is illustrated in figure 4.1.

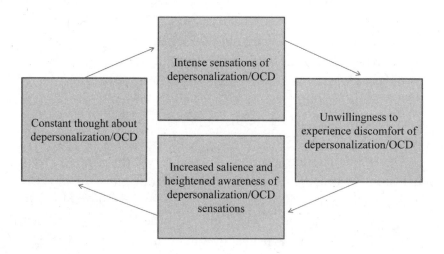

Figure 4.1 Reciprocally Reinforcing Maintenance of Depersonalization/OCD Symptoms

Cognitive defusion is an acceptance-oriented therapeutic strategy that allows you to see thoughts as just thoughts—as an output of the brain—that are constantly generated and won't be quieted. Adopting a perspective in which you don't buy into the content of your thoughts is considered useful for managing relentless, nagging, or obsessive thoughts. Chapter 6 elaborates on this technique. Also, obsessive thoughts often imply a disastrous consequence. For example, you may have the thought, "Depersonalization is so awful. I'm going to have to feel this way forever." A disastrous consequence you may fear is a life in which you are totally alone, alienated from people, totally brain-dead, or unresponsive while you live in a residential mental health facility. You may fear that you will reach a point when DPD will keep you from being able to articulate your discomfort, when you will be a burden to your family, or when your spouse will leave you. Many fears underlie the obsessions of chronic depersonalization, and exposure to these disastrous consequences may help you face your fears about depersonalization. Chapter 8 elaborates on exposure techniques.

Borderline Personality Disorder

Borderline personality disorder (BPD) is an enduring condition associated with interpersonal conflict; extreme, rapid mood swings; impulsivity; a tendency toward dangerous or risky behaviors; chronic feelings of emptiness; and a tendency to see things in very black-and-white terms (seeing things as being either entirely at one extreme or another), among other criteria. Feelings of emptiness and the experience of not knowing yourself are observed in both BPD and DPD. People with DPD demonstrate *self-objectification*—sensations that the environment is rapidly changing, the line between the self and the environment is unclear, or both (Jacobs and Bovasso 1992); this is reminiscent of the disturbed self-image that's characteristic of BPD. Also, *emotion dysregulation*, which means difficulty with emotionally appropriate behaviors, and inconsistent emotional reactions are observed in both disorders. Furthermore, early childhood trauma (most specifically, sexual abuse) is a predictor of both DPD and BPD.

In people with BPD, emotion dysregulation is often observed as trouble responding appropriately to intense emotions, which can sometimes manifest as volatility, hostility, or panic. Dialectical behavior therapy (DBT) (Linehan 1993a) offers specific strategies for regulating emotional reactions and tolerating discomfort. Many of these techniques may be useful for managing symptoms of depersonalization. Chapter 7 introduces DBT skills.

Affective Disorders

Depersonalization is frequently misdiagnosed as depression. It's easy to see why; people with depersonalization often say they can't get excited about activities they used to enjoy. This can easily be mistaken for *anhedonia*, a loss of interest in previously pleasurable activities, which is a common symptom of depression. People with both depersonalization and depression have difficulty concentrating. However, inattention in depression tends to be related to preoccupation with distress, while inattention in DPD has more to do with perceptual disturbance and difficulty integrating information. Basically, this means that people with DPD tend to have a difficult time taking in a lot of information at once; even familiar environments may seem overstimulating and overwhelming. You may feel unable to make sense of what you are seeing, even though you can recognize on an intellectual level what your senses pick up.

People with depression and people with DPD both relate somatic symptoms (bodily discomfort with no identifiable physical cause). If you are preoccupied with bodily sensations, you will make your physical discomfort worse; you may become obsessed with your physical symptoms, and the more you obsess, the more you will focus on the negative experience. So, in other words, DPD is characterized by inordinate attention to bodily, emotional, and cognitive (thinking) experiences of discomfort. Attention to discomfort tends to make discomfort worse; again, it's easy to see the irony and inconvenience of this vicious cycle.

It's no surprise that a majority of people with DPD also meet criteria for an affective disorder (for example, dysthymia, major depressive disorder, or bipolar disorder). So it's not always easy to distinguish depersonalized symptoms from depressive symptoms. People with DPD are often depressed, but it's fair to say that distress over symptoms of depersonalization contributes to depression. Likewise, symptoms of depression also exacerbate symptoms of depersonalization, because excessive or prolonged distress can sometimes elicit symptoms of depersonalization. People with DPD often relate that their negative ruminations are almost entirely composed of worry about their ability to live long-term with debilitating depersonalization and the immediate discomfort of symptoms. So, it's typically concluded that depression may follow depersonalization, rather than the other way around. This is further confirmed by the fact that among people with co-occurring depersonalization and depression, depression tends to wax and wane, while symptoms of depersonalization remain constant and unwavering.

SUMMARY

Episodic depersonalization may be useful for all of us, because it allows us to manage extremely stressful situations with numb, detached composure, but some people develop chronic depersonalization, which may last for years and years. The exact cause of chronic depersonalization (DPD) isn't always clear, but people who develop it tend to have endured a traumatic experience or unyielding emotional discomfort of some sort, or may link the onset of depersonalization to drug use (such as marijuana, ecstacy, or ketamine).

Depersonalization and other dissociative experiences are extremely common in many psychological disorders, such as panic disorder, post-traumatic stress disorder, borderline personality disorder, obsessive-compulsive disorder, and mood disorders. Given the fact that emotional overload frequently precipitates a depersonalization response, it makes sense that you may experience DPD in conjunction with a mood or anxiety disorder.

We briefly introduced a few therapeutic strategies throughout this chapter. In future chapters, we'll elaborate on these techniques, giving you specific strategies for managing unpleasant feelings related to depersonalization. Acceptance-oriented and behavioral techniques will be the predominant focus of chapters 6, 7, and 8. As you proceed, complete the provided exercises, because you'll derive the most benefit if you are actually *experiencing*, rather than just learning about, the therapeutic techniques.

5

Depersonalization from an Acceptance and Commitment Therapy Perspective

Whenever we introduce a relatively new form of acceptance therapy called acceptance and commitment therapy (ACT) to the people who come to our clinic for help, we're met with some resistance and a little bit of annoyance. Their response almost seems to be that not only do we not understand their suffering but we are also now asking them to accept it: "How dare you ask me to accept my suffering, my discomfort! You're not in my shoes. I would like you to live like me for a day and tell yourself to accept living in anxiety and despair all day." Of course, this is not what we are asking people to do. We are merely stating that human suffering is part of life and that sometimes struggling against it or constantly looking for an end to it just keeps perpetuating the suffering, thereby intensifying it. If you are like the people we work with who have DPD, what we are asking you to do is to stop struggling day in and day out, and to try to live your life. Okay, easier said than done, but we will show you how.

Acceptance has recently received a great deal of attention in terms of managing psychological discomfort, and a major way acceptance strategies differ from traditional cognitive strategies relates primarily to how unpleasant thoughts and feelings are handled. Psychotherapeutic approaches have historically referred to "healthy normality," meaning that when people are psychologically healthy, they are happy, peaceful, calm, and motivated to pursue healthy opportunities. The corresponding assumption of this idea is that sadness, anxiety, and discomfort are evidence of some kind of mental illness. On the contrary, acceptance therapy approaches believe that suffering and discomfort are not only normal and part of life but also necessary for the survival of the individual and the species, because they alert us to sources of threat. Rather than being evidence of illness, emotional discomfort is part of living with fluctuating levels of distress throughout your lifetime. The acceptance approach suggests that many of us rely too much on our emotions to guide our behaviors, thus perpetuating a life of unhappiness.

Acceptance-oriented therapies strive to dismantle the power that we frequently allow emotions to have over our choices, because they can sometimes lead us astray. At one time or another, you have probably neglected to do something that was important to you because you didn't "feel like it." Ultimately, it's easiest to let your feelings guide you, but if you take an honest look, you may be able to see how this kind of reasoning can contribute to psychologically dysfunctional behaviors. For example, why would someone who's experiencing depersonalization choose not to go to work? Maybe because he feels overwhelmed by discomfort or depression, feels a sense of cognitive fogginess when professional responsibilities are expected of him, or is nervous about what he might say in a depersonalized state when interacting with colleagues throughout the day. Notice that discomfort, depression, and nervousness are all emotions, and in this example, the person is giving them control in terms of guiding his behavior. Acceptance-oriented therapy seeks to undermine the power we give to emotions when we make important life decisions, because while emotions can be informative, they don't always properly represent what's best for us. In the example just given, it's easy to see how going to work may be the best thing for this person, while yielding to the emotional urge (staying home from work) will only lead to more dysfunction. We certainly understand, however, that the emotional impulse may be difficult to resist.

Emotionally guided behavior is not exclusive to experiences of depersonalization; this is a trap that everybody falls into every day. To relieve her embarrassment, a mother might choose to buy a toy for her child who's throwing a tantrum in a public place; an employee might choose to take on extra work to avoid an awkward discussion with his boss about work limits; a child might not do her homework because the material is too difficult and frustrating for her. In these examples, again notice that embarrassment, awkwardness, and frustration are all emotions that are guiding people away from the most appropriate (and, ultimately, rewarding) activities.

The point is that there's nothing inherently pathological about this process (we all do it, and it's obviously a somewhat natural response for humans), but when it gets out of control, it can keep you from staying engaged in life (for example, avoiding work or social relationships, neglecting personal responsibilities, or all of these). Also, allowing your emotions to guide your behavior can make feelings of depersonalization worse. The reason for this is that feelings of depersonalization are increased during periods of self-focus and rumination. What do you think you are likely to do if you are not interacting with people, not going to work, or not fulfilling mundane responsibilities, such as going to the grocery, bank, or department of motor vehicles? If you are like most, you will likely sit at home and think about your DPD, how awful things are, and how unpleasant the future will be. The question is not whether these feelings are legitimate; the question is whether or not they are urging you in the right direction. Are they helpful?

In a nutshell, practicing acceptance will teach you to be *willing* to experience discomfort, because it's a natural by-product of a rich existence. And, while your experiences are legitimate and feelings of depersonalization are intensely uncomfortable, techniques discussed in subsequent chapters will help you to evaluate whether your behaviors are serving DPD or a valued, purposeful existence. We'll explore specific techniques for managing unpleasant feelings so you can stay engaged in life, despite your emotional or experiential ups and downs, including feelings of depersonalization.

Depersonalization According to ACT

Acceptance and commitment therapy (ACT) (Hayes, Strosahl, and Wilson 1999) is one of the most widely practiced acceptance-oriented therapies used today. Many of the concepts and techniques explored in this book relate directly to ACT principles and research conducted by leading ACT theorists, including Stephen Hayes, Kirk Strosahl, and Kelly Wilson. An elaborate explanation of ACT is beyond the scope of this book, and interested readers should refer to *Get Out of Your Mind and Into Your Life* (Hayes and Smith 2005). However, the following section will explore ACT principles and how they relate to experiences of depersonalization.

According to ACT, psychological dysfunction is composed of six core processes that contribute to an overall orientation, landing somewhere on the continuum of psychological flexibility to inflexibility. *Psychological flexibility* refers to willingness to experience a range of sensations, emotions, and thoughts, as well as to engage in a variety of activities, all of which contribute to a rich life that's peppered by discomfort as a natural consequence of staying engaged in important life activities. For example, if you are willing to feel somewhat alienated in a romantic relationship, you will pursue a romantic partner and reap the benefits of companionship, while tolerating the interpersonal discomfort associated with DPD. Of course, the alternative to this is nothingness: no experiences, with no corresponding discomfort but also no benefit or achievement. If you decided not to experience detached affection (as is commonly described by people who experience depersonalization), then you will begin to limit the types of experiences you will allow yourself to have. You may avoid romantic situations, you may avoid conversation with prospective partners, and you may hold out for the day when depersonalization goes away, all the while squandering the only thing that's truly real: the present moment and present opportunities. It's easy to see how you could lose years of potential experiences in the process, all because of your refusal to feel unpleasant feelings. Furthermore, rigid patterns that are established over years are difficult to reverse, so even if depersonalization does eventually go away randomly, you may find yourself so accustomed to a rigid or avoidant lifestyle that being engaged in your life is a foreign practice, inspiring discomfort in and of itself.

According to ACT, the litmus test for psychological functioning is not how good you *feel* but, rather, how willing you are to endure a range of experiences, both pleasant and unpleasant. It follows that we may be better able to see how we are doing psychologically, based on what we *do*. Emotional urges may tempt us to do things that are not in the interest of our well-being (for example, avoiding social situations due to feelings of depersonalization). The goal of increasing psychological flexibility is not to make emotional urges go away but, rather, to adjust the power we allow them to have over

us (in other words, acting according to what's in our best interest rather than according to what our emotions want us to do), a
concept illustrated in figure 5.1. Next, we'll look into the six specific
qualities that contribute to a generally inflexible orientation.

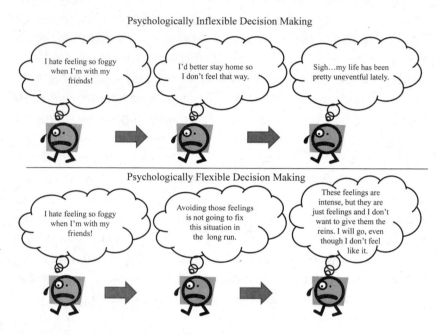

**Figure 5.1 Psychologically Inflexible Decision Making
Juxtaposed with Flexible Decision Making**

Cognitive Fusion

Cognitive fusion is when you buy into what your mind presents
to you. In reality, every thought and feeling you have is a reflec-
tion of electrochemical reactions and learned associations that exist
in their purest form on a neurological level. As human beings, we
can't possibly see things in a purely objective manner. However,
everything you know, you saw through the filter of your mind; you

don't know any other type of reality. So it's hard to combat the importance your mind places on its own observations and interpretations. Cognitive fusion simply refers to the natural tendency of the mind to present its content as gospel. Your mind has you believe that everything it shares with you is 100 percent accurate, from the color of the grass to the devastation that will ensue following a breakup. The evolutionary reason for this is clear: if you don't believe what the mind shows you, you might not react when you are faced with a dangerous situation. Cognitive fusion is a really important survival mechanism. However, it can also guide us in the wrong direction when it comes to emotional problems. When the mind tells you, "I feel totally hopeless," cognitive fusion provides this implied amendment: "There must be no hope for the future; things must be very dismal if I feel this way." In other words, because the mind thought it, it must be true and very important.

Even if your thoughts are "true" in some sense of the word, the attention you may give to them isn't necessarily useful. Most people with DPD are terrified by their perceptual symptoms and are constantly uncomfortable. The reality of this discomfort may be "true" as much as something can be, but the focus or attention and rumination that are frequently afforded to these symptoms are more unhelpful than helpful. The fact that people with DPD frequently deliberate on their symptoms has a great deal to do with fear that the symptoms are evidence of something more serious (dementia, "losing your mind," totally losing control, and so on). So it's fair to say that cognitive fusion is at work here: the mind, which is constantly alarmed by the unusual perceptions of depersonalization, believes that these perceptions are vitally important and require immediate attention. Because you buy into the thought that your feelings resulting from your DPD are important and need to be focused on, you are vulnerable to dropping everything and becoming totally paralyzed when DPD feelings and thoughts come up. It's clear how this can ultimately deplete your quality of life.

To make matters worse, when you are emotionally uncomfortable, you are likely to engage in unhelpful behaviors, such as avoidance or aggression. Referring again to the example of the man who wants to avoid DPD-related "fogginess" in social situations, the emotionally guided response would be to avoid what brings about discomfort. It's easy to see why this might lead to increased suffering in the long run.

Identifying "You" from Your Beliefs About Yourself

You may find that you try to define yourself according to your thoughts: "I am obsessive," feelings: "I am depressed," labels: "I am depersonalized," and evaluations: "I am a good person." Notice how all these sentiments include the verb "am." Essentially, this locks you into a role: if you *are* depersonalized, there's no way to feel or act in opposition to this label. On the one hand, it's hard to imagine that there's a distinction between *you* and the activities of your brain. After all, your evaluations, interpretations, and feelings about things are basically inseparable from how you experience the world. But, on the other hand, how can you *be* the content of your thoughts and feelings if they are so vulnerable to change? Think about it: you were wrestling with different problems and concerns this time last year. This time last night, your mood was probably at least slightly different. Over time, sometimes you're laughing, and sometimes you're crying. Sometimes you're thinking about your grocery list, and sometimes you're thinking about the meaning of life. If the content of your mind is so subject to change and so vulnerable to so many things (for example, disappointment, a good night's sleep, the weather, exercise, and so on), isn't it fair to say that the you that's really *you* is found somewhere underneath all of that cognitive activity, that there's an aspect of you that's more constant, more level?

If you see yourself as defined by the content of your thoughts, you'll tend to let those thoughts and labels guide your decisions, and you may be more likely to act according to what your mood is urging. Because, after all, if you *are* depersonalized, what's the point of trying to be anything else? In other words, if you identify yourself entirely by feelings of depersonalization, it's hard to see yourself in any other role. According to the *DSM-IV-TR* diagnostic criteria, people with DPD experience impaired functioning with regard to social or work pursuits (or both), or functioning in some other major life area. Therefore, if you have DPD, you *have* to be impaired, which is a view of yourself that may not motivate you to engage in difficult activities. And a similar conclusion may be inferred for all labels you impose on yourself; it's hard to be flexible and try new behaviors when you already know who you are and what limits you. The more invested you are in these thoughts and labels for yourself, the more they may restrict you, locking you into certain roles and practiced behaviors, which may ultimately contribute to inflexibility and a stifled routine.

Rumination and Worry

Rumination and worry take us out of the present moment. People with depersonalization (or any psychological distress) tend to be very focused on things that aren't necessarily relevant to what's going on in front of them at this very moment. We mentioned earlier how rumination, a term used to describe a digestive process in cows whereby food is returned to the mouth to be chewed again, also describes a habit of thinking whereby ideas, concerns, focus on failure, and so on are brought relentlessly back to consciousness for contemplation. It wouldn't even be so bad if you were just constantly aware of DPD-related discomfort, but you are probably also constantly plagued by what this feeling means, what's "wrong" with you, what the doctors have missed, whether you'll ever get better, what you can do to make yourself better, what treatments might be helpful, and so on.

This kind of thinking would also not be so destructive if it ever resulted in any relief, but it only seems to make things worse. Think back to the five most recent things you might have ruminated on. Write them down and then, next to them, write down how ruminating was helpful. Did it help you to solve a problem or accomplish something constructive? Did your efforts bring you to any conclusions or solutions? Did you have any insights that you didn't already have? Did relentless thought about your situation make you feel any better? If you are like most people with depersonalization, the answer to these questions is probably no. Now, think back over the years you have been struggling with depersonalization and applying this type of thinking to make yourself better. Has it worked? Unfortunately, as we mentioned, you can't simply stop ruminating just because you want to; the mind is notoriously resistant to instruction. As we go forward, we'll introduce ways to manage relentless focus on distress and reorient your attention to the present moment.

Experiential Avoidance

Experiential avoidance is anything you do to avoid or escape unpleasant internal experiences. An unpleasant internal experience is an emotion, thought, or sensation that causes significant discomfort. If you are afraid of speaking in public and refuse to speak to a group of people, it's fair to say you are avoiding the scenario, but it's also fair to say that you are avoiding the anticipated thoughts and feelings that will result from participation (for example, anxiety, perception of negative evaluation from the audience, and so on). Experiential avoidance can be as blatant as not leaving the house or as subtle as using methods to distract yourself from thinking about something unpleasant. Self-medicating using alcohol is a good example of how methods of experiential avoidance may eventually serve a counterproductive function: while the immediate result of experiential avoidance is relief from discomfort, the long-term result is, at best, stagnancy and, at worst, abuse or dependence. Furthermore, experiential avoidance may perpetuate psychological dysfunction.

People who suffer from depersonalization describe many unpleasant internal experiences, including lack of mental clarity, difficulty elaborating on feelings, and sensory disturbance (for example, numbness, distrusting their own sensations, and so on). Avoidance inevitably leads to inflexibility and restriction of activities, which may ultimately prevent you from achieving your goals. If you avoid situations that provoke depersonalization, it's likely that something important will be neglected at some point, that you may not be able to live your life according to your values, and that you will continue to suffer. For example, if you can't focus at work, you may begin to pull away from work-related responsibilities, and it's easy to see how you may ultimately pay for this.

Furthermore, depersonalization may, in and of itself, represent a form of experiential avoidance, because you feel numbness in place of the extreme emotions that would otherwise overwhelm you. As discussed in chapter 1, the mind may impose depersonalization as a means of distancing you from extreme emotions during emotionally evocative experiences. In a manner of speaking, this is a survival mechanism that malfunctions in certain people.

As we'll discuss in greater detail in later chapters, adopting an orientation of *willingness* to experience discomfort may be the only way to break this cycle. Because you have depersonalization and will experience sensations of it regardless of whether or not you *want* to, willingness to experience it while engaging in value-driven activities will only allow you to live a richer, more fulfilling life, while experiential avoidance will only compound feelings of guilt, inflexibility, and acknowledgment of missed opportunities. When we begin to outline practical strategies for overcoming the negative impact of depersonalization, we'll introduce activities to increase your willingness to experience a range of emotion, both pleasant and unpleasant, which will help to combat experiential avoidance related to feelings of depersonalization.

Lacking Clarity of Values

According to ACT, *values* are "chosen life directions" (Hayes and Smith 2005, 154). Values are *chosen* because they are conscious and deliberate, and they're demonstrated through your behavior; they are *life directions* because they help guide behaviors. ACT frequently refers to values clarification as "setting the point on the compass" (ibid., 155), meaning that through determining your core values, you can set a direction and prepare yourself to pursue it, seeing specific milestones down the road. While you are leading a life based on your values, you can achieve many goals; values, however, differ from goals in that you can never fully attain values. Values direct your behaviors, but they don't take you to a final destination, whereas goals do direct your behavior to a final destination. For example, if success within an intimate relationship is a value for you, you can never truly stand back and say, "Ahh, now that that's taken care of, I don't have to worry about it anymore." You are never *done* satisfying a romantic partner, and you are never *done* attaining a value. Values merely provide us with the blueprint for how to live our lives. Another example is that if you value having a career, you will engage in all behaviors that are necessary to attain a career, succeed at your career, encourage others to get careers, associate with people who have careers, and so on. Your goal may be getting a particular job that symbolizes success in a career. The former is value driven and never ending, while the latter is a final destination (getting the job).

If you don't have a clear sense of what's important to you, it's easy to see how certain difficulties may arise. Because discomfort and preoccupation with internal experiences tend to dominate the lives of people with DPD, they may lack clarity of values. If this is the case, it becomes hard to see what you are living for. This isn't meant to sound morbid; rather, when someone is experiencing depersonalization, it's easy to get wrapped up in the thoughts, feelings, and motivations that come with depersonalization; the focus on what's *truly* meaningful to you can get lost. We'll more specifically address forming clear values in chapter 6.

Narrow Behavioral Repertoire

Committed action (which will be introduced in greater detail in chapter 6) is a voluntary action that reflects what's truly important to you. If intimate relationships represent a valued life area, committed action on this value might be planning some special activity with your spouse or partner. If a fulfilling career is a value for you, committed action on this value might mean going back to school.

The flip side of committed action, of course, is a *narrow behavioral repertoire*. People who have a narrow behavioral repertoire are not allowing their values to guide their behaviors. If you valued creativity but didn't pursue creative activities, you would be demonstrating a narrow behavioral repertoire. When asked, people with DPD usually cite various reasons for not pursuing activities that are important to them because of their discomfort in certain situations which inspire unpleasant emotional and perceptual experiences. However, when these sources of discomfort are allowed to guide your behavior, the range of behaviors you are willing to experience becomes narrowed, and stagnancy inevitably follows.

ACT METAPHOR:
Passengers on the Bus

Following is a classic ACT metaphor that conveys the struggle of living with enduring unpleasant emotional experiences and the toll emotionally guided decision making takes on flexibility (Hayes, Strosahl, and Wilson 1999, 157). The question to consider as you read on is: "Am I living for myself, or am I living for depersonalization and other psychological discomfort? Who exactly has control of the wheel?"

Imagine you are a bus driver with a full load of passengers, each of whom represents some aspect of discomfort you experience. One passenger may represent your inability to tap into your emotional experiences, one may be your attention or concentration difficulties, one may be your sense of lack of contact with reality, and so on. Each passenger is big and mean looking, and walks to the front of the bus to shout in your ear, but they can't cross the yellow line (they can't actually take control of the wheel).

Now imagine that the passengers insist you make only left turns. Left turns represent things the depersonalization asks you to do or not do in its service (for example, avoiding interactions with others, avoiding work responsibilities, avoiding chaotic or unpredictable circumstances, and so on). As long as you make only left turns, the passengers keep silent in their seats. But if you decide to make a right turn, the passengers get up and shout at you, making their feelings heard (for example, through your experience of mental "fogginess," emotional or physical numbness, and so on). So, to appease the depersonalization passengers, you are careful to make only left turns. And for some time, this solution placates the volatile passengers, but soon enough, you are making only left turns and driving in circles. Depersonalization is restricting your range of experiences because it has very little tolerance for intense emotions.

Now imagine that you decide you are tired of living your life in circles, so you start making right turns. The passengers shout and make obscene gestures, even threatening you or making you feel sad. But ultimately, you've got control of the steering wheel, and as long as you are willing to hear whatever they shout at you, you can take the bus anywhere you want to go. You are free to do what's in line with who you are and who you want to be. In short, this is what we call psychological flexibility, which, as discussed previously, means being open to experience a range of emotions as you pursue things that are important to you.

As this metaphor suggests, acceptance can help you live the life you choose. Your suffering is intense, and it's hard to imagine being willing to experience it. But meanwhile, waiting for things to get better and trying to force things to get better have still left you in pain and waiting. Depersonalization is all blow and bluster; though it will make you incredibly uncomfortable, ultimately it *has* to yield to where you choose to carry it.

SUMMARY

This chapter examined depersonalization with ACT principles in mind. We described the six core dysfunctional processes that have facilitated your discomfort:

- Cognitive fusion

- Identifying "you" from your beliefs about yourself

- Rumination and worry

- Experiential avoidance

- Lacking clarity of values

- Narrow behavioral repertoire

The interaction of these factors contributes to an orientation of psychological inflexibility, with the overall pattern of trying to avoid unpleasant feelings, and consequently avoiding important life areas. Those areas of life that we tend to value the most are the areas that are limited the most. Therefore, depersonalization may contribute to an inflexible routine where not only discomfort is limited but also richness and diversity of experience. As we proceed, we'll discuss ways to ensure that valued life areas aren't neglected, even *while* feelings of depersonalization persist. Chapter 6 will examine the flip side of these dysfunctional processes, helping you establish an orientation of willingness and acceptance.

6

Using Acceptance and Commitment Therapy

Now that we've supplied you with some ACT tools, we'll teach you how to use them. Once you've begun to use ACT, you'll start living a more meaningful life. According to ACT, psychological inflexibility interferes with your moving forward in your life. So increasing flexibility will increase your mobility in life, allowing you to participate in activities that are important to you. According to ACT concepts, you can do this by targeting the six qualities we discussed in chapter 5. Each dysfunctional process corresponds to a functional process that you can start to foster. For example, the opposite of experiential avoidance is willingness to experience discomfort (anything that might be internally uncomfortable, such as depersonalization, anxiety, a perceived negative social evaluation, a chilly shower, the burn of overworked muscles, or bereavement). If you are willing to experience sensations and feelings you wouldn't ordinarily enjoy, then you can behaviorally put yourself into contact with them. For example, if contact with a specific person makes you feel more depersonalized, your willingness to interact with that person forces you to feel the depersonalization you have been avoiding. Each corresponding process is introduced next, with practical solutions for fostering a more functional approach.

The Functional Approach: Doing What Works Rather Than What Feels Right

Life is full of experiences that range from inconvenient to traumatic, amusing to euphoric. Sometimes it seems that things *should* be different, that things aren't right and something has to change for you to be able to move on. And while this sits well with your sense of justice, it's not always the most useful way of approaching situations. For example, a man with depersonalization wants his feelings for his wife to return so that when he hugs her again, he'll really *feel* the feelings that usually accompany such an act of intimacy. Trying to hug his wife without "feeling it" doesn't feel right for him; it feels as if he's lying. He worries that hugging his wife might even make the depersonalization more pronounced (in that his awareness of his numb feelings will be more evident when doing something that normally evokes emotions). However, it's not hard to see why hugging his wife, despite his lack of feeling, might actually be in his best interest: his wife may feel that he's letting her in, so she'll validate his effort and soften to him. Consequently, he might feel heard by her and feel more connected to her as a result of having a shared experience. The end result of demonstrating affection, despite his lack of feeling, might be that he *does* wind up feeling the affection he's been holding out for. Even if his feelings don't change in any way, his wife might feel and appreciate that he tried, which might make her more willing to do what she can to help him. She may be more willing to ride out the difficult times if she gets the impression that he's considering her need for affection. His commitment to *acting as though* he has affectionate feelings for her might just save a troubled marriage.

This example basically includes all the important aspects of psychological flexibility. In this case, acting against his feelings shows that the man *values* his relationship with his wife, even if his feelings aren't always engaged. Though he experiences discomfort when acting against what his feelings tell him to do, he *accepts* these unpleasant feelings. And finally, he shows affection for his wife, demonstrating *committed action* or *value-driven* behavior. This chapter explores these and additional ACT skills. The strategies discussed next are intended to allow you to adopt an accepting disposition and tolerate the discomfort that sometimes accompanies living according to your values.

Cognitive Defusion: Managing Unpleasant Thoughts, Feelings, and Sensations

As discussed in chapter 5, because the mind is extremely sensitive to information in the environment that may indicate vulnerability to some threat that's present, it's hard for most of us to imagine that the mind would lie to us. Our first reaction to a thought is "What can I *do* to fix or improve this situation?" This fix-it mentality can become a problem for many people who find themselves overwhelmed by symptoms of depersonalization, because thoughts are often hopeless and feelings distressing.

As you'll recall from chapter 5, cognitive defusion refers to getting a little distance from thought processes. Even though your thoughts can reflect "true" dangers, at the end of the day, they are just thoughts, and taking them literally all the time can lead to suffering that compounds suffering. For example, you can think about exactly what it would be like to have a bear gnaw on your leg (the sound it might make as it rips your tendons, the sight of your blood pumping out of your arteries as they are severed, the feeling of the bear's teeth hitting your bone, and the pressure of tugging as soft tissue separates from hard tissue). Maybe you felt disgusted as you read this, because your mind can represent thoughts as if they were real. You can experience some semblance of the feeling you would have if a bear were really gnawing on your leg. So even if there's no bear and no danger, your thoughts can "stand in" for reality. This skill is unique to human beings; and while this has been so beneficial for us in terms of abstract thought and creativity, it can do us a tremendous disservice when it comes to thoughts about things with emotional resonance. In the same way that buying into the bear imagery can lead to disgust, buying into thoughts about your own worthlessness can lead to despondence. For this reason, it may be helpful to adopt a position of watching your thoughts unfold, rather than absorbing everything your mind says as if it reflects the only reality.

ACT makes a distinction between observing your thoughts (cognitive defusion) and observing *from* your thoughts (cognitive fusion). When we are *fused* with thoughts, we see no distinction between thoughts and reality, and the mind runs rampant, making judgments, evaluations, and interpretations, which we then buy into wholeheartedly. So in other words, if you have a thought and believe it reflects reality, it's pretty impossible not to act according to what your mind urges you to do. However, if you have a thought and see it as just a thought (just something the mind generates), you have more flexibility; you don't necessarily have to act in accordance with it. The goal of cognitive *defusion* is to give us a bit of room in this process so we can recognize and *experience* thoughts as just thoughts, without necessarily having any bearing on the external environment or our actions. Cognitive defusion requires deliberate effort because it doesn't come naturally, and your mind (which wants you to believe what it says) will make this clear when you practice the following exercise.

It may be difficult to distance yourself from troubling thoughts and feelings of unreality, because emotional discomfort is primarily the result of perceptual disturbance. John, one of the people with DPD described in previous chapters, once articulated this concept perfectly: "If you had never been depressed a day in your life and someone dropped you in a very deep hole in the middle of the desert, you would eventually get depressed." Basically, the despondence you experience when you are depersonalized is at least partially due to the extreme, chronic perceptual discomfort, which may not always have much to do with negative thinking. However, the negative-thinking by-products of these perceptual disturbances may be targeted using cognitive defusion. For example, if you have experienced depersonalization for an extended period, you may ruminate for hours on end about how uncomfortable your experiences are, how unpleasant the future will be, and how impossible life will become if you continue to feel this way. Similarly, you may also obsess about the meaning of your condition, what neurological damage you may have, what treatments are available, and the meaning of life in general. Therefore, thought-observation strategies and cognitive defusion techniques may allow you to get a little distance from the troubling, relentless thoughts that tend to compound the discomfort of the perceptual disturbance.

MEDITATION: Leaves in a Stream

This is a classic ACT exercise that's intended to give you a little "cognitive breathing room," allowing your mind to do whatever it does, while you focus on the *experience* of thinking, rather than getting caught up in the specific content of your thoughts (Hayes, Strosahl, and Wilson 1999, 158). This exercise involves immediately observing each thought, one after the other, as it occurs to you. As ACT authors Kelly Wilson and Troy DuFrene (2008, 13) refer to this process, you just "watch the show" your mind performs. The show will go on no matter what: your brain will comment, reflect, try to solve problems, and criticize. Your only task is to try to watch as this inevitable process unfolds. The purpose of this exercise is to notice whenever there's a shift from looking *at* your thoughts to looking *from* your thoughts. You'll know this has happened when you find you are no longer engaged in the exercise but are following some train of thought. Though the process of observing your thoughts is relatively simple to explain, you'll soon see that it's almost impossible to maintain.

Imagine yourself standing over a stream, looking down at the water as the current carries it from one side of your field of vision to the other. Just try to hold onto this image for a minute, and get a feel for the speed and rhythm of the flow. Now imagine that floating in the current are leaves that are being carried downstream one at a time. One by one, the leaves enter and leave your field of vision. Now imagine that each thought that occurs to you is being projected onto a leaf as it passes. As a thought comes to you, let it fall into the stream and float away with the current. When a thought passes from one side of your field of vision to the other, let go of that thought and make room for the next one.

Your task is to just watch the flow of leaves, without making it stop and without jumping down into the water and chasing a thought downstream. Just let the current flow. It's very unlikely, however, that you can do this without interruption, which is the key part of this exercise. At some point, you'll have the sense that the stream has stopped or disappeared, that you've lost the point of the exercise, or that you have floated downstream with a thought instead of just observing it from the riverbank. When that happens, back up a few seconds to see if you can catch what you were thinking or feeling right before being carried away. Then go ahead and imagine your thoughts on the leaves again until the stream disappears a second time, and continue this cycle. Your main objective is to notice when the flow stops for any reason, and to see if you can catch what happened right before it stopped. Notice how the thoughts that pull you off course are often thoughts associated with problem solving, rumination, and/or obsession about things that are troubling.

Transcendent Sense of Self (or the "Observer Self")

After completing the previous exercise, you may be led to question the difference between being the observer of thoughts and buying into your thoughts. When you observe thoughts, you are tapping into the "observer self." This is an aspect of you that has been with you your whole life. While you have always had thoughts, feelings, and experiences while interacting with your environment, you have also had an awareness that you were observing, that a part of "you" was just taking notice. You were able to practice this experience in the previous exercise, but it has been with you your whole life. See if you can acknowledge this aspect of yourself right now. Think about the present moment, what you are currently doing and where you are at this moment, and see if you can simply notice noticing. The following meditation is intended to allow you to tap into the transience of most things we tend to observe, including things we tend to identify with the "self": the labels, evaluations, and emotions we use to define ourselves. The purpose of this exercise is also to acknowledge that you can have an experience without that experience defining "you." For example, if you see a chair in your field of vision, this is an observation, something acknowledged by the mind. Likewise, you can probably observe an emotion in your own consciousness. Even though the emotion feels more personally relevant to you, it's still just an observation of the mind;

it's no more "you" than the chair you can observe. Read through the following meditation a few times to memorize the instructions, and then guide yourself through the meditation to help distinguish between "yourself" and what you observe.

MEDITATION: Self as Observer

Following is another meditation based on *Acceptance and Commitment Therapy: An Experiential Approach to Behavior Change* (Hayes, Strosahl, and Wilson 1999, 192).

Bring your attention to your surroundings. You may be sitting down with this book in your hand. Look around you; what do you observe? There may be windows and furniture in your view, or you may be outdoors; just take notice of what's around you and realize that there's a distinction between what you are looking at and the "you" that's looking. Just try to feel the line that's drawn between "you" and the world. Just pay attention for a minute to the experience of observing.

Now turn your attention to the objects you are immediately touching: maybe you can feel the book in your hand or the chair, bed, or ground that supports you. Notice the distinction between these objects you are immediately interacting with and the "you" that experiences them. Just notice for a minute the sensation of objects you are touching.

Now notice your body. We are now getting closer to objects that are personally relevant to you. Your body is yours, but it's not "you." Notice that you can tap into cues sent to you from different parts of your body; notice that "you" are observing your body. Again, notice the distinction between the body that you feel and see, and the "you" that's observing. For a minute just concentrate on what it feels like to feel your body and any sensations your body informs you of.

Now turn your attention to your feelings and thoughts. You have a great deal of personal investment in them, and they may have given you a lot of grief as you have tried to manage your experience of depersonalization. Just like cues from your body, your thoughts and feelings inform you of things that may be important for you to know. Notice that, like your body, your thoughts and feelings are not "you." Notice that you can experience your thoughts and feelings, and notice the "you" that's noticing. Again, notice the distinction between the thoughts and feelings you experience and the "you" that experiences them.

Turn your attention to your firmly held ideas about who you are, what traits you possess, what roles you fulfill, what type of person you believe you are, and so on. This is how you typically describe yourself, and you may be very invested in these self-concepts. Notice that you can feel like an "honest" person, an "isolated" person, or a "worthless" person. Notice how you may be more or less invested in these labels at different moments. Sometimes you are a "student," sometimes you are a "daughter," sometimes you are an "employee," and sometimes you are a "patient." Notice how each of these roles is situation specific, that the only constant here is something in you that underlies the transience of thoughts, feelings, roles, self-concepts, and scenery. See if you can notice the distinction between what you believe about yourself and the "you" that believes.

Finally notice the "you" that's the point from which all of these observations are made. It's the only place that can truly be called "here" or "now." It's the point from which you observe. It's your point of reference, and it's the only thing that has remained constant throughout your whole life—not the objects in your environment, not your body, not your thoughts or your feelings, not even your roles or your strongly held beliefs about yourself. The only thing that stays with you through all of it is the "here" or "you" that's observing. Therefore, rather than the "self" being the content of your experiences (environment, thoughts and feelings, sensations, beliefs, and so on), maybe it's truer to say that "you" are the context of your life, the context where all of this stuff plays out.

Notice that all of the things you've been struggling with and trying to change are not you anyway. See if you can let go just a little bit, aware of the knowledge that you have been "you" through everything you have been through, and that you need not have such an investment in all this psychological content as a measure of your life.

Mindfulness: Living in the Moment

Mindfulness basically means being present to your experiences while you are experiencing them. When you drive all the way to the store with no memory of how you got there, this is an example of mild dissociation. Most people experience dissociation of this variety when they mindlessly complete activities or are lost in thought for some length of time. Dissociation for people with chronic depersonalization goes beyond this, because the ability to focus on immediate awareness is the very mechanism that's impaired. Emily, one of the people with DPD presented in chapter 1, used to say that when she looked at a familiar scene, it seemed as though she were seeing it for the first time. She said she couldn't "tap into" or concentrate on the scene, that everything seemed foreign and unfamiliar, and that perceptions were always fuzzy and detached. To make matters worse, *trying* to focus on things just brought attention to her impaired perceptions, endlessly frustrating her. Her experience suggests that, although mindfulness is frequently used as a therapeutic technique, it may be exceptionally difficult for you. Also, since thought content is often negative, this can be a very painful process. As previously discussed, you may find it difficult to put down the process of chaotic thought, because one unpleasant interpretation follows the last.

However, because it represents a central area of difficulty, mindfulness is also a crucial skill to be fostered. As discussed in chapter 5, rumination and worry can be detrimental because there's nothing you can do to remedy mistakes you made in the past, and beyond basic planning, there is little that can be done to correct problems that have yet to come. So when we spend a good deal of time lost in thought, we have missed the only moment we had any hope of experiencing. Developing mindfulness skills may help you contact unpleasant feelings in a spirit of willingness, allowing you to experience sensations (rather than interpretations of sensations) while redirecting your focus (and cognitive judgment) back to your sensory experience. We'll introduce specific mindfulness strategies for managing depersonalization in chapter 7, which introduces another acceptance-oriented treatment, dialectical behavior therapy (DBT) (Linehan 1993a).

Acceptance and Willingness

The approach of engaging in life despite discomfort doesn't initially sit well for most people. A common sentiment is "I shouldn't *have* to do it without feeling it; I shouldn't *have* to live this way; I just want it to go *away!*" And as true as this is, ask yourself whether it's helpful, whether your refusal to act as a matter of principle is moving you in the right direction.

When you are willing to engage in a range of experiences (even if you experience them in a numb way), you open yourself up to all of the possibilities life can offer. Susan, introduced in chapter 2, recalled a period of true isolation and avoidance in almost all of the important areas of her life. Essentially, life was too overwhelming for her if she had to remain in a state of chronic depersonalization. Her life became lonely and unfulfilling because she was confined to her bedroom in an effort to avoid the discomfort related to depersonalization. With avoidance and waiting for relief motivating her choices, his life stood for little more than survival and tension reduction. And while discomfort associated with depersonalization is not the average person's experience, suffering is. Suffering is a natural by-product of putting yourself out there and caring about something (for example, you're bound to encounter disappointment, self-consciousness, and rejection if you engage in the things that are meaningful to you).

Many people with depersonalization (or any psychological discomfort) are searching for ways to make the feelings go away. But feeling good doesn't necessarily translate to psychological health. To illustrate this point, it may be helpful to imagine how chasing positive feelings can sometimes get in the way of your overall well-being. For example, drug addicts make a lifestyle out of trying to banish unpleasant feelings while inviting only pleasurable ones; it's easy to see the toll this may take on an addict's well-being. And while this represents an extreme example, everyone tends to employ this type of agenda. Giving a speech is something most people find pretty intimidating, and prior to giving a speech, everything in your body tells you to get out of the situation immediately (an example of the fight-or-flight reaction). But this response is generated by a primitive and emotion-driven part of your brain, and deliberate thought allows us to behaviorally override this urge. Deliberate thought might lead you to go through with the speech despite your discomfort. And essentially, acceptance is just that: willingness to experience discomfort as you go through with activities that have value to you. There are consequences to getting involved in important activities when you live with depersonalization. The unpleasant consequence of going to a party may be a baseline feeling of disorientation and alienation, but the benefit of socialization may be meeting new people or sowing the seeds of a relationship. This type of discomfort is the "stuff of life." We can only be truly peaceful in life if we are moving toward accomplishment in the areas of life that are important to us, and we can only do this *while* enduring the discomfort of depersonalization.

Values

So if you decide you aren't going to allow your emotions to steer you away from what's important to you, what will guide you?

Your personal values can give you a guide for action that's less vulnerable to fluctuation, more predictable, and more constant. You can understand values as the point that's set on the compass. A value isn't a specific accomplishment on the horizon but, rather, a direction you travel in because it's inherently meaningful to you. Clarifying your values helps you identify those areas of life that need more attention. If you really think about what your thoughts and actions are focused on, relative to what you truly value in life, you'll probably see some discrepancies. For example, depersonalization requests inordinate attention from you when it wants you to listen to it as it explores reasons and treatments for your suffering or when it wants you to go to myriad doctors, seeking tests for obscure neurological conditions. Cognitively and behaviorally, it wants *all* of you. Meanwhile, you may have children, a spouse, a passion for painting, a vacation coming up, and a rare collection of records, among other life investments that rank as truly meaningful to you. And even though depersonalization is *not* meaningful to you and you are trying desperately to get rid of it, ironically it takes up so much of your time and energy. The following exercise is intended to show you life areas that you may value but possibly neglect. Attention to such discrepancies will conceivably help you make choices that are more in line with what you want your life to stand for, rather than what depersonalization urges you to do.

EXERCISE: Choose Your Values

This exercise is intended to determine your valued life areas and how successfully you have been living by your values. Ultimately, it will help you direct your attention to areas that need more of your focus and time. Anyone can find this table useful, because we can all improve our lives through self-reflection and committed action.

In the "Importance" column, rate how important each valued area is to you on a scale of 1 to 10 (where 1 indicates low importance and 10 indicates high importance), and in the "Success" column, rate from 1 to 10 how successfully you have pursued each area (with 1 meaning very unsuccessfully and 10 meaning very successfully). Discrepancies are relevant; for example, if you place the importance of an area at 1 and your success in that area at 9, this is an area to focus on. Feelings of depersonalization tend to interfere with interpersonal functioning, but work, academic, and hygienic or health functioning may also be affected. This table will allow you to identify areas that are important to you but are being neglected.

Value	Importance 1–10	Success 1–10
Parenting		
Marriage or Intimate Relationship		
Other Family Relations		
Friendships or Social Relations		
Career or Employment		
Education, Training, or Personal Growth		
Citizenship		
Recreation or Leisure		
Spirituality		
Health or Physical Well-Being		
Other:		
Other:		

A Valued Lifestyle + Acceptance = Committed Action

Once you have clarified your values and identified neglected life areas, where do you go from there? Clarifying your values leads directly to a discussion of *committed action*, which basically means behaving according to your values. In the earlier example, if the man with depersonalization values a relationship with his wife, it doesn't matter whether or not he feels an urge for intimacy; he can follow a valued course regardless of his feelings (or lack of feelings). Going back to the "passengers on the bus" metaphor in chapter 5, you have ultimate control over your actions, even if your actions are accompanied by emotions that urge you to go in a different direction. Unpleasant feelings are likely to come up along the way if you are following a valued course, because the long-term payoff of committed action isn't always as immediately alluring as short-term satisfaction. Again, referring to the earlier example, the unpleasant feelings that accompany intimacy might urge the husband to isolate himself, while the valued response would be to behave intimately, guiding him toward marital satisfaction. Therefore, it's necessary to adopt an accepting disposition with regard to the unpleasant by-products of committed action.

SUMMARY

This chapter summarized the central themes of acceptance and commitment therapy (ACT), with an emphasis on managing depersonalization. We discussed the importance of doing what works as opposed to doing what feels right. We suggested accepting your discomfort while staying engaged in life, as an alternative to waiting for depersonalization to go away. We summarized the six functional processes of ACT:

- *Cognitive defusion* was introduced as a strategy for approaching unpleasant thoughts that targets the influence we allow our thoughts and feelings to have over our behaviors.

- The *observer self* represents the aspect of you that has observed every thought, feeling, role, interest, and phase of physical development you have undergone. Tapping into your observer self helps you maintain focus on the transience of your emotional experiences and the ebb and flow of life in general.

- *Mindfulness* refers to being immediately aware of what you are experiencing. This is an important skill that's difficult for people with depersonalization to foster due to the perceptual disturbance that's common. Mindfulness strategies will be explored in greater detail in chapter 7.

- *Willingness and acceptance* is the opposite of avoidance. Being willing to endure and accept emotional pain is necessary to pursue anything of value in life.

- Clarifying your *values* allows you to base your life choices on more than what "feels right." Values are less susceptible to change than are emotions or thoughts. They represent important areas of your life that can serve as your direction for the life choices you make.

- *Committed action* refers to pursuing behaviors that are in line with your values, with a spirit of acceptance and of willingness to experience the discomfort that may arise in the process.

Acceptance of discomfort leads seamlessly into a discussion of behavioral strategies for combating depersonalization, because behavioral approaches are most effective when you completely throw yourself into the activity with an attitude of willingness (for example, not avoiding your emotions while you participate in exposure exercises).

7

Using Dialectical Behavior Therapy Strategies

In this chapter, we'll discuss another acceptance-oriented approach, called *dialectical behavior therapy* (*DBT*) (Linehan 1993b). DBT was originally developed for people with borderline personality disorder (BPD), a disorder characterized by extreme emotional volatility, recklessness or impulsivity, and relationship problems. Many people with BPD say they experience episodes of depersonalization, which isn't surprising, given that extreme emotional discomfort can bring on depersonalization. Likewise, as discussed in chapters

1 and 2, chronic depersonalization itself is extremely uncomfortable, which may lead to emotional volatility and emotion-driven decision making, two tendencies DBT specifically targets.

DBT focuses on behaving deliberately, tolerating distress, and acting with mindful awareness of what you are experiencing and what's best for you. Many of the techniques included in DBT are useful for treating DPD, including mindfulness and distress-tolerance techniques. This chapter will briefly explore the basic concepts of DBT as they relate to DPD, and we've included a few DBT exercises to help manage the discomfort of DPD. However, because an in-depth understanding of DBT concepts and strategies is beyond the scope of this book, if you are interested in further study, refer to *The Dialectical Behavior Therapy Skills Workbook: Practical DBT Exercises for Learning Mindfulness, Interpersonal Effectiveness, Emotion Regulation, and Distress Tolerance*, by Matthew McKay, Jeffrey C. Wood, and Jeffrey Brantley (New Harbinger, 2007).

We know DBT works for people with BPD, who, like those with DPD, express feelings of numbness, unreality, and inability to connect to others. Because feelings of unreality and numbness are the central experiences of DPD, you, too, can benefit from learning to regulate your emotions and tolerate your distress.

The Dialectical Approach

In philosophy, *dialectic* refers to the clash between arguments and counterarguments. The aim of the dialectical method is to resolve the disagreement through rational discussion and, ultimately, the search for truth. The idea is that you can derive the truth as contradictions arise. Each movement forward is a consequence of our reaction to the contradictions inherent in the preceding movement, which is just a fancy way of saying that it's the dialectic that moves us forward, the synthesis of the thesis and antithesis. Well, all of this may sound like a bunch of intellectual banter. For us, it suffices to say that it's the synthesis of our intellect and emotions that allows us to keep developing and behaving in the healthiest manner (Linehan 1993b).

Dialectics also recognize that two opposite ideas can be simultaneously correct. In philosophy, dialectical arguments use logic but don't necessarily imply absolute truths. In other words, two opposing viewpoints can be equally "correct" based on frame of reference and personal values. This idea is clear in any political or other controversial issue; for example, your position on something like abortion or taxation is based on not only logic but also your personal values. The reason we disagree about things often boils down to what can't be *proven*.

DBT helps people foster recognition of dialectical experiences in life to help combat black-and-white thinking (Linehan 1993a). Fostering dialectical awareness helps people see the black in the white and the white in the black. Note that this doesn't involve seeing "shades of gray." It's not about finding a compromise between two opposing concepts but, rather, a synthesis of the two. You can be insecure and arrogant at the same time, or you can be simultaneously numb to your experiences and miserable about them, which is another dialectic your loved ones may have a difficult time understanding. Logic can't always make sense of a situation, and emotion doesn't always lead you to the most appropriate action, but both logic and emotion must necessarily interact with each other to achieve balance (Linehan 1993a). We will describe a few common dialectics next.

Rational vs. Emotional Mind

Paradox is unavoidable in a balanced life. The most powerful example of this is the interaction of our rational mind and our emotional mind (Linehan 1993a). The rational mind seeks solutions to problems, and thrives on finding absolute truths and universal experiences. On the other hand, the emotional mind rejects rules and acts on emotional impulse. Your emotional mind helps you pursue passions or avoid discomfort, and while these actions may bring relief in the short term, they can be destructive in the long term. For example, anxiety, discomfort, or fear of experiencing feelings of depersonalization may lead you to avoid certain social or work responsibilities. Feeling that your concentration is impaired may lead you to avoid mentally taxing activities, and sensitivity about appearing "out of it" may cause you to avoid conversation. In a sense, when you avoid life because of DPD, your emotional mind is in control.

Both your emotional and rational minds are vital to your psychological health, which is why we are all equipped with both (Linehan 1993a). If you weren't passionate about things, you would be unaffected when bad things happened to you, you wouldn't protect your loved ones, you would have no preference for one thing over another, and essentially, you wouldn't be you. If you weren't equipped with a rational mind, you would be a frantic, emotional whirl, pursuing every impulse without concern for consequence. Though these two forces are sometimes at odds, they have to somehow come up with some solution that satisfies both for you to achieve a well-balanced life. If permitted, intellect and emotion *can* coexist, even though they are fundamentally opposed; they just need to reach a synthesis, a solution that grows out of this contradiction. DBT refers to this synthesis as *wise mind* (Linehan 1993b). Wise mind incorporates intuition into this equation, which allows people to behave reasonably with regard to emotionally intense experiences. Wise mind allows you to see and experience events calmly, which allows for awareness of the whole picture.

When the emotional mind is too much in control of your life and you can't handle intense emotions, you are *emotionally dysregulated*. In an emotionally dysregulated state, you not only feel miserable but also feel as if you can't achieve your goals, and you may feel injured or alienate yourself from others; everything just seems to go sour in your life.

It may be that you had trouble responding to intense emotions (that is, you were emotionally dysregulated) prior to developing DPD, and perhaps developed DPD to protect against your reactions to strong emotions. Maybe feeling emotionally out of control was too frightening. Your ability to tolerate discomfort had worn thin, leading you to shut down and protect yourself by becoming numb and disconnected. However, this protective reaction wasn't very effective, and it led you to once again experience extreme negative feelings of anxiety and depression—but this time, over the experience of DPD. You couldn't tolerate feeling numb and disconnected, being unable to concentrate, feeling unable to bond with others, and not knowing when relief would come. Your preoccupation with these feelings and your quest to get rid of them, once again, gave rise to more difficulty dealing with emotions and an even lower distress tolerance. You have likely found yourself on an emotional roller coaster and in a vicious cycle.

Related to DPD, emotional dysregulation may involve avoidance of situations that elicit feelings of depersonalization or discomfort in general. Occasionally, people with depersonalization may engage in extreme efforts to "feel something," such as cutting and other forms of self-mutilation. Cutting and other self-injurious behaviors are not the best way to get rid of numbness.

Fostering wise mind can lead to *emotional regulation*, which simply means developing the ability to deal effectively with your emotions; we'll discuss how to do this later in this chapter. When it comes to DPD, emotional regulation is important because it's all too easy to let extreme anxiety and depression take control and then to become focused only on your internal emotional state. DBT skills help regulate your emotional state.

Acceptance vs. Change

Another important dialectic involves the interaction of *acceptance* and *change* (Linehan 1993a). In our discussion, to accept means to adopt a peaceful disposition related to emotional pain, while change implies avoidance of emotional pain. In acceptance you allow the pain to accompany you as you try to go on with your life. In change you take action to reduce your pain by either changing your belief system or avoiding the discomfort. According to DBT, like other dialectics, acceptance and change need to find a synthesis. As we discussed in previous chapters, acceptance involves being willing to experience an uncomfortable feeling and, at the same time, continue living your life according to your values. Change, on the other hand, involves seeking ways to reduce your discomfort.

The clash of acceptance and change gives rise to emotional dysregulation. You may wonder why this is so. Think for a moment: if you feel numb or robot-like, and that makes you anxious, how can you be willing to experience the numbness and anxiety, and simultaneously be unwilling to experience it? From willingness and unwillingness has to come a third option, which might be turning your focus away from your internal state to that of the external world. You will notice that this option is neither avoiding your discomfort nor succumbing to it. Through retraining your attention, you find a synthesis—and a solution for dealing with DPD discomfort.

The Misery of DPD vs. Feeling Numb

We can also view the experience of depersonalization in terms of dialectical balance. Many people with DPD describe themselves as "numb," but this isn't exactly the case, or at least it's not the whole picture. "Numb" implies indifference. When you go to the dentist and are given Novocain (procaine), your nerves are indifferent to any drilling that's being done to your teeth. Emotional numbness or a completely flat disposition may be better diagnosed as a thought disorder or another condition where acknowledgment of reality is impaired, rather than depersonalization. People with depersonalization tend to be very emotive but have difficulty identifying, perceiving, or interpreting their emotional experiences, all the while remaining tragically aware of how wrong it feels, which may lead to panic or despondence. Numbness represents one facet of what it feels like to be depersonalized, but this aspect of DPD has equal counterparts. Ultimately, feelings of numbness are troubling only because of intense passion (rather than indifference) for connectedness, clarity, and work or social success. This concept relates back to the discussion of values and pain introduced in chapter 6 (we experience pain and fear only about things that are meaningful to us; two opposing feelings are corresponding aspects of the same coin, and it's impossible to get rid of only one side).

Mindfulness

A core skill of DBT is *mindfulness* (Linehan 1993a). Mindfulness, which was also a central theme of chapter 6, refers to being in the present. The goal of mindfulness is to attend to what *is* rather than how things *appear* to be. Mindfulness exercises, like the one that follows, encourage you to focus on immediate experiences, direct sensations, and events as they unfold. This generally involves breaking habits of automatic responding and, instead, observing everything you do and feel as you do and feel it. If you have DPD, this can be an anxiety-provoking experience, because you may feel as if you can't properly perceive sensations or feelings. You may also get caught up in wondering whether your feelings are, in fact, coming from you. Don't be afraid to experience the frustration and discomfort that may come along with this practice. Rather, just acknowledge the unpleasant emotional reaction as you would any other immediate experience. The trick here is to *just observe* without judgment. And remember, mindfulness is not about *getting* anywhere; it's about merely acknowledging where you are and what you experience, including thoughts, feelings, sensations, evaluations, information provided by your body and mind (such as pain and your interpretation of it), and information provided by the outside world (such as the light from a lightbulb or the sound of cars outside).

EXERCISE: Introduction to Mindfulness

Though mindfulness is a meditation technique, you can apply it almost anytime. In fact, it's important to practice it in everyday situations, especially during emotionally evocative experiences. You can practice these strategies right now, as you read this book, and that's how we'll begin:

1. Balance the weight of your body evenly across your spine, and straighten your back. Notice how, through a feedback process, you can sense your equilibrium and adjust your posture based on that sensation. Sit comfortably with this book in your hands and your hands in your lap.

2. Notice the feeling of the chair, bed, or couch below you. Notice where the chair touches your body, and just concentrate for a minute on the sensation of this pressure. Notice how the chair supports your weight, that gravity pulls you to the earth, and that the chair stops you. Think about what a tremendous force gravity is, that we are constantly being pulled down. This is a sensation you can tap into, but probably rarely pay attention to. Notice the feeling of the ground beneath your feet and the sensation of any other object your body is in contact with.

3. Now turn your attention inward. As you did with sensations associated with objects in your environment, you can tap into sensations of signals your body sends you. Notice what it feels

like to breathe. The muscle that controls each breath you take is your diaphragm, located just below your lungs. Notice how your diaphragm contracts and how the suction this creates rushes air into your lungs; notice that the air is cool as it hits the back of your throat and travels down your trachea. Just feel the sensation of breathing; breath is the rhythm of your life, anchoring you to the present moment. Notice how you rarely attend to the sensation of breathing unless you feel something unpleasant, like being out of breath or needing to cough.

4. Now see if you can notice your heartbeat. If you are really quiet and inwardly aware, you can tap into the feeling and even the sound of your own heartbeat, which also marks your time as a living creature. For a moment, just notice the sensation and what your heartbeat means for you as a human being. Notice how the only time you think of your heartbeat is when it indicates something distressing to you, like anxiety or vigorous exercise. Notice how, this, too, anchors you to the present moment.

5. Notice that there's an ebb and flow to breathing (an inhalation and an exhalation), just as there's an ebb and flow to your heartbeat (contraction and expansion). Your whole body operates this way; your thoughts, feelings, and sensations are all in process, with nothing standing still. Think about how this cyclical pattern is an aspect of life on this planet: highs support and are supported by lows. A life without either will contribute to stagnancy.

Though these instructions may initially seem a little silly to you, you can use them to help ground you during periods of extreme discomfort. Depersonalization is, more or less, a failure to tap into your immediate awareness, so mindfulness allows you to give time to each of your experiences *as you experience it*, taking one at a time. Mindfulness helps you accept your discomfort, because nothing seems truly insurmountable if you are concentrating on only one thing at a time. *Awareness* is the only goal here. We don't expect you to be able to achieve total peace, or to be totally happy about depersonalization or any other discomfort you face on a regular basis. Actually, the more you strive for total peace, the more elusive it will be. The goal here is to witness your life as it unfolds. This skill doesn't come naturally to us, because we tend to default to automatic reacting; it's very foreign to do things deliberately and with awareness. And while automatic responding helps you do things quickly and easily, it also leaves you stuck in your mind while ruminating on the discomfort associated with depersonalization. This process can make your experience of depersonalization worse, because perceptual discomfort is compounded by worry about what that discomfort means, leading to increased suffering and disruptions to living a healthy lifestyle.

Mindfulness allows you to focus on one thing at a time, breaking down each of your experiences into a single observation. If you were about to clean your house, you would likely feel more overwhelmed if you thought all at once about everything you had to do to accomplish this goal: "Not only do I have to clean the bathroom, but I also have to wash the dishes, mop the floor, vacuum the carpets, and make the beds." However, if initially you *just* clean the bathroom or, better yet, *just* scrub the sink, you'll do *just* that, until it's time to move on to the next thing. A mindful lifestyle implies treating all of life in this manner: concentrating on just one experience at a time. As a consequence, life will feel less overwhelming, because your only task is to be in *this* moment; when the next moment arrives, your only task is to experience *that* moment, and so on. The overall result is that you'll be able to tolerate being in the present, being engaged in every aspect of your activity of the moment, and being mindful of all your actions and surroundings, rather than letting yourself get carried off into the past or future.

EXERCISE: Acting Mindfully

Mindfulness is about more than having a quiet, inward focus. You can practice mindfulness when doing just about anything. Practice this technique during the most mundane or meaningful activities. The following list is only a sampling of activities you can do with your attention on one sensation at a time. Try using mindful awareness when:

- Brushing your teeth

- Taking out the garbage

- Hugging your spouse

- Driving to work

- Crying

- Walking

- Eating a meal

You can apply your mindfulness practice to any experience, from eating a bowl of oatmeal to dealing with losing a loved one. There's literally nothing that you can do where mindfulness is impossible. Using awareness on a regular basis will help you feel your feelings without letting your mind carry you away. Many guides are available to help you master this skill. *Full Catastrophe Living*, by Jon Kabat-Zinn (Delacorte Press, 1990), is an excellent introduction to mindfulness; the concepts we discuss in this book were originally adapted by Kabat-Zinn for people with chronic medical conditions. You can seamlessly apply many of these concepts to your situation, because the perceptual experiences of chronic depersonalization are as uncomfortable, unrelenting, and unreasonable as the discomfort of a chronic medical condition. *Going to Pieces Without Falling*

Apart, by Mark Epstein (Broadway Books, 1999), is another excellent introduction to the use of mindfulness practice and philosophy to manage suffering. This book talks about dealing with challenges in life with mindful awareness, and accepting the feeling of being overwhelmed as you endure the ups and downs.

Chapter 8 will introduce behavioral strategies for managing feelings of depersonalization. You can seamlessly apply mindfulness skills to behavioral strategies. As you practice the exercises described in chapter 8, try to stay present to what you feel. Your mind will likely try to distract you from your feelings, or pull you into an elaborate reaction to your discomfort; for example, "This feeling is so uncomfortable. Why is this happening to me? Where can I possibly go from here?" Try to redirect your awareness to *just* the feeling, rather than what the feeling means or what it implies for the future.

Distress Tolerance

Developing mindfulness skills contributes to an overall attitude of acceptance of reality, which will help you tolerate distress (Linehan 1993a). Life is full of pain for everyone, although the magnitude of the pain is certainly different for different people. When you have depersonalization, unfortunately life is very painful, and most people have no idea what you are going through. Because there's not much anyone else can observe, you probably don't even get a lot of sympathy or compassion. You probably feel alone and isolated because no one sees what you are going through. It's so hard to even explain your world, the reality you live in day in and day out. Because your reality is an altered sense of most people's reality, it makes total sense that you would want to get out of your reality and into the reality of others, though it has been impossible so far. We hope that by the time you've finished reading this book, you'll have started living a healthier and more valued life.

Reality doesn't necessarily need to be changed or manipulated. As we already know, your reality is not ideal. You may suffer daily with discomfort, fear, depression, and feelings of unreality; you didn't choose this outcome, nor did you choose many of the life circumstances you're stuck with. Nonetheless, you are here, and the only thing you can do is the best you can under the circumstances. Life can be likened to a game of cards in which you have to take certain chances and encounter risk. Chance and uncertainty are what make games worth playing and life worth living. A good player who's playing a card game merely for the experience of the game wouldn't want to be able to choose how the cards are dealt. The deck is dealt, and the hand that's given to you is the hand you must play. You have choices about which cards to hold versus which ones to trade, and you can choose when to fold or when to raise the stakes. There are options for *how* to play once the cards have been dealt, and the best thing to do is use your judgment and make reasoned decisions about how to play the game. You may not have a choice about what your hand looks like, but you do have a choice about what you do with it. Acceptance of the hand you've been dealt is necessary for you to play the best hand you can. Mindfulness fosters acceptance, and accepting the reality of your life allows you to tolerate the distress and ambiguity of the game. If depersonalization is a particularly unfavorable hand you've been dealt, accepting this reality will allow you to do your best at life, despite the additional challenges associated with depersonalization. We realize accepting your situation is far easier said than done, but daily mindfulness practice will help you establish a more accepting disposition toward depersonalization discomfort or any other of life's struggles.

Suggestions for Developing Distress Tolerance

When you feel particularly overwhelmed or panicked due to depersonalization or other sources of distress, it may be useful to change the emotional scenery. Note that we are referring to *change,* rather than *acceptance* strategies, in this section. The whole point is to break the emotional cycle to bring about a different internal climate. Distress-tolerance skills include distraction, self-soothing, and focusing on one thing in the moment (Linehan 1993a). *Distraction* is as it sounds: drastically changing your emotional experience by doing something that will cause less distress and awareness of feelings associated with DPD. *Self-soothing* involves engaging in activities that will calm you or redirect your focus onto things that have deep or spiritual meaning for you. And *focusing on one thing in the moment* is using mindfulness to calm yourself down. Basically, this involves bringing your attention to something in the environment outside your internal chaos. Here are a few activities that may help to calm you down when you're feeling particularly overwhelmed by DPD or any other discomfort:

- Watch a favorite or familiar movie.

- Take a long walk.

- Sprint down the block until you nearly collapse from the exertion.

- "Take a break" from a troubling issue or argument.

- Pray (if you consider yourself religious or spiritual).

- Train in a relaxation technique.

- Do something engrossing and enjoyable (such as playing with your dog, knitting, woodworking, or cleaning).

- Deliberately notice colors in the room or sounds you would ordinarily ignore (for example, cars passing outside or the sound of the air conditioner). When your mind tries to draw you back into the chaos of your internal dialogue, just keep bringing your focus back to what you can observe in the external environment.

Emotion Regulation

DBT is frequently used to help people who experience intense emotional urges that may be very destructive to act on. When these emotional urges come on, DBT helps arm you with more-productive ways to neutralize them (Linehan 1993a). As discussed previously, depersonalization can guide you toward emotionally reactive behaviors as you attempt to overcome it, so it's important to learn how to resist these responses. To help you resist such urges, you might find emotion-regulation skills useful, because resisting DPD-related behaviors (for example, avoidance of emotionally evocative situations) can be extremely uncomfortable (Linehan 1993a). Many emotion-regulation techniques are available within the DBT literature, and if you're interested, refer to a self-help book that provides a more comprehensive introduction to all that DBT offers (see Recommended Reading). For the purpose of this book, we'll address a few specific strategies that are most directly related to the struggles associated with depersonalization.

Acting Against the Urges of Depersonalization

Acting against emotional urges (Linehan 1993a) means doing the opposite of what your emotions want you to do. We'll explore this concept in greater detail in chapter 8, which examines behavioral strategies for managing depersonalization. Therefore, the following will be only a short synopsis.

When someone has social anxiety, the emotional symptom of anxiety is reinforced by the behavioral symptom of avoidance of social situations. So, to stop feeling unpleasant emotions, you have to let yourself be in situations where those unpleasant feelings will be evoked. If you can feel the emotional urge (such as to skip the party) but do the opposite of what the emotion wants (such as go to the party anyway), the magnitude and strength of the emotion will decrease over time. Also, if you consistently see that your fears represent no legitimate threat, your alarm reaction will relax a bit (for example, parties won't seem quite as threatening).

Think about what depersonalization has urged you to do or not do. Maybe you resist seeing certain people who make you feel particularly numb, maybe you neglect certain mentally taxing activities because of the feelings of confusion you experience, or maybe you resist starting a meaningful romantic relationship for fear of lacking "genuine" romantic feelings. Opposite action implies doing what you would do if those fears and feelings weren't a factor. Of course, you don't have to take the most difficult opposite action immediately, but kind of work yourself up to it. So, for example, if mentally exerting activities cause you extreme discomfort because of depersonalization, doing your taxes on your own may seem incredibly difficult. To break down this difficult and anxiety-producing task, first take the action of paying your bills or organizing your paperwork. As mentioned, we'll cover this concept in greater depth in chapter 8.

Breaking Through the Fog by Naming Internal Experiences

The experience of depersonalization carries with it a *disconnect*, or a difficulty integrating emotions, sensations, and thoughts. As a person with depersonalization, it's not unusual for you to feel as though you are removed from your feelings. The ambiguity of emotional and sensory experiences can lead to added discomfort. This is why the first step is to know what you are feeling and give it a name. DBT therapists often say, "If you can name it, you can tame it," and this idea is useful for people with depersonalization (McVey-Noble, Khemlani-Patel, and Neziroglu 2006). Mindfulness about emotional experiences will help you become more aware of and better able to label them. You can do the following mindfulness exercise when you feel particularly emotionally unanchored, confused about your emotional experiences, or both.

MINDFULNESS EXERCISE:
Labeling Your Emotional Experiences

There are a couple of ways to do this exercise: you can either complete each instruction as you read it, or first read through the set of instructions and then guide yourself through each step from memory.

1. Get in a comfortable position and take a deep breath. As you breathe in, feel the air travel deeply into your lungs and abdomen, all the way down into your stomach.

2. Briefly bring your attention to each area of your body, and notice the feeling of the weight of your body as it sinks deeply into the furniture that supports you.

3. Notice any sensations you experience in your body, focusing on one area at a time.

4. Bring your attention to your emotional experiences as they occur to you. Often, depersonalization causes people to worry that they'll get carried off into the atmosphere and lose their footing emotionally. Naming each feeling as it comes to you makes each experience of that feeling a bit more concrete.

5. For each thought that occurs to you, try to determine the emotion underlying the thought. Think about that feeling and call it by name.

6. Continue attending to your thoughts and labeling any feelings accompanying those thoughts for five to ten minutes.

You'll recall John, one person we were able to work with, from earlier chapters. During sessions, he frequently said he needed a "road map" to his emotions, that he sometimes felt so out of control that he had lost the ability to discern one strong feeling from another. He often described himself as "emotionally confused." During sessions we tried to focus on basic external and internal information he recognized, without judging or making efforts to change those experiences. We completed the previous exercise and asked John to verbalize his reactions to the instructions. Following is a series of excerpts from that exercise:

John: "I notice how quickly my mind tries to bring me back into that endless dialogue. My mind resists 'just observing.'

"It's weird, because I can feel what my feet feel like. It's strange to just feel that without needing to for some reason.

"I'm feeling foggy. This is difficult 'cause I feel like I'm trying to think...but thinking isn't the goal here....I'm feeling foggy."

Therapist: "Sit with 'foggy'; just notice what this feels like."

John: "I'm feeling depressed because I'm so foggy. I can't imagine how this will make me feel any better. I'm very sad about what DPD has done to me.

"I just thought how scary it is that I don't know what's going on with me. Is it DPD, or is it something more neurologically systemic?"

Therapist: "And what emotion underlies this?"

John: "Fear, anxiety, panic...."

After the meditation, we discussed whether the urges associated with fear, anxiety, fogginess, depression, and panic would lead John toward what would be best for him. We were able to determine what emotions guided his behaviors, whether these behaviors were in line with his chosen direction, and, if not, what alternative actions he might adopt deliberately. Though just a summary of the often-difficult process of determining emotions and acting against them, this is a good example of how mindfulness (immediate awareness of emotional experiences) may lead to deliberate action rather than emotionally guided action.

Emily also participated in the previous exercise; she described the following experiences:

> Attention to internal information can sometimes feel overwhelming, especially when I feel more depersonalized—although focusing on one area at a time without judgment was a bit unusual for me. When I usually monitor how I feel, my observations are usually followed by rumination about their meaning. During the exercise, redirecting my attention to my sensations was helpful; I felt that it kept me grounded. Labeling my experiences and redirecting my mind every time it tried to wander helped me stay present to my experiences, even if they weren't particularly pleasant.

Interpersonal Effectiveness

Interpersonal effectiveness skills are important for everyone to work on. *Interpersonal effectiveness* means balancing your needs with those of the people you interact with, being tactful in representing your needs, and using an assertive communication style (Linehan 1993a). If you experience depersonalization, you may often encounter relationship problems because numb feelings *about* relationships are disturbing to you and your friends or family members. John expressed great fear that the numbness he experienced would lead him to constantly doubt his feelings in relationships, resulting in permanent isolation. John's thoughts on this issue capture the interpersonal consequence of DPD:

More than anything, I'm afraid of what I'll miss out on in life because of this condition. I've had many relationships that have ended the same way: in the past, girlfriends loved and appreciated me, and wanted to get closer to me, but I was generally unmoved by them. And while I can't tap into many feelings in the moment, I'm acutely aware of and depressed about what I've missed out on in life. Sometimes I feel like I'm just not getting the point of life, that everyone else has been let in on it and I'm the only one deprived of a real sense of meaning.

Furthermore, during his marriage, John's wife frequently acknowledged his depersonalization, even though the couple didn't consciously talk about his condition; to describe the emotional shift she observed, she often said he was "disappearing." John became increasingly more troubled by his own symptoms and frustrated by her acknowledgment of them, which led to reoccurring conflict in their relationship.

This isn't an uncommon scenario. Chronic DPD may make you feel as if you have a difficult time tapping into your feelings during emotional experiences, and that may be distressing to loved ones, who see you as "aloof" or "robotic." Likewise, if you try to explain your emotional experiences, you may receive unsupportive reactions, because depersonalization is a frustrating and elusive concept for people who have never experienced it. Meanwhile, people with DPD need to have their feelings validated. It may feel helpful and bring relief to hear a loved one tell you, "I can't imagine how bewildering this must feel for you. Based on what you've told me, I think anyone in this situation would be just as panicked or despondent as you are." Validating statements such as these would probably help you feel that you've been heard and help you feel more connected.

If you are in a relationship, your partner may feel that his needs aren't being met, which, of course, leads to relationship struggles where both of you are upset and dissatisfied. Assertive communication can help you reconnect. Assertively communicating your feelings of depersonalization may help improve your relationships with your family members, too. *Assertiveness* involves reasonably and calmly representing your feelings with "I" statements, acknowledging how the other person feels, and seeking a solution. Expression of *feeling* is the goal here: talking about how you feel rather than how things *are*. As the person asserting your feelings, it's your responsibility to *tactfully* express yourself. Emily frequently engaged in heated arguments with her parents about the pain she experienced related to depersonalization. The following dialogue, which comes from a family session held with Emily and her parents, demonstrates a couple of communication failures. First we'll relay the dialogue as it happened, and then we'll explore a more assertive solution Emily and her parents might apply during such a discussion.

Emily: "I'm not going to get better; I just can't imagine how I can go on this way."

Emily's father: "But you're not *trying*. I've put so much money into treatment—not to bring up money, but you don't seem to put any effort into it."

Emily's mother: "Emily, we've been at this for the longest time. I don't know what this depersonalization business is about, but first you thought you had obsessive-compulsive disorder, then you thought you had bipolar disorder, then borderline personality disorder, and now depersonalization. I get that you're trying to figure out what's wrong with you, but how many labels do you need before you actually make some changes?"

Emily: (to therapist) "What am I supposed to say to this? [crying] I don't know how to make this go away. If my brain is damaged, I don't know how this will ever get better. Then I have to listen to *this* [gestures to parents], which doesn't make things any better. Like *this* is helping me feel more connected? I just want to die."

Mother: "Emily, don't say things like that."

Emily: "What if it's true? If this feeling doesn't go away, I can't imagine how I'll tolerate life."

Father: "That's absurd, Emily; you have so much to be happy about. It could be so much worse."

Emily: "This is *bad*, Dad! I just don't think you care to understand that."

Both Emily and her parents are guilty of emotion-guided communication, aggressiveness, and invalidation. Let's take a closer look at what went wrong. Remember, the goal here is to communicate feelings, but without judging or violating other people.

Emily began by saying, "I'm not going to get better; I just can't imagine how I can go on this way." What Emily is really saying is that she feels incredibly hopeless and desperate. Assertively communicating these feelings, rather than speaking in absolutes ("I'm not going to get better"), will help her parents better understand what she's struggling with.

Emily's father responded, "But you're not *trying*. I've put so much money into treatment—not to bring up money, but you don't seem to put any effort into it." This invalidating statement wasn't the most helpful observation, nor was it necessarily accurate. A more assertive (and more accurate) way to express his frustration might be something to the effect of "I feel frustrated with the situation, too; I only want you to get better and feel better."

Emily's mother then said, "Emily, we've been at this for the longest time. I don't know what this depersonalization business is about, but first you thought you had obsessive-compulsive disorder..." These statements are also invalidating. Emily's mother is expressing frustration about the unreliability of diagnosis and the ambiguity of Emily's feelings in general. It may have been more useful for Emily's mother to validate Emily's frustration with her own, telling Emily that she's also upset about Emily's suffering and the mixed clinical messages from mental health professionals.

Emily then said to the therapist, "What am I supposed to say to this? [crying] I don't know how to make this go away. If my brain is damaged, I don't know how this will ever get better. Then I have to listen to *this* [gestures to parents], which doesn't make things any better. Like *this* is helping me feel more connected? I just want to die." Emily's sadness is evident in these statements. She's afraid she will never recover, she fears a permanent loss of connection, and she feels that her parents are only exacerbating the interpersonal numbness. It's important for her to express her feelings about this in a way that doesn't come across as combative. It would be assertive for Emily to say, "I feel uncomfortable when you imply that this is somehow my fault, and I feel more alienated from you when we argue about my condition like this. I understand that you're frustrated and think I'm not trying. Maybe the best thing for me to do is to tell you every day what I've tried from the suggestions my therapist has given me, to show you that I'm really trying."

EXERCISE: Practicing Assertive Communication

1. Go over the last four lines of the previous dialogue and see if you can think of assertive responses to replace the unproductive, invalidating, and aggressive ones in the original dialogue.

2. Consider the impact unassertive communication may have had on your life and on your feelings of depersonalization.

3. Reflect on a recent interaction or argument that unassertive communication may have affected. What might have been a more assertive way to approach it?

SUMMARY

This chapter examined dialectical behavior therapy (DBT) principles and exercises (Linehan 1993a). The dialectical approach involves accepting ambiguities and logical contradictions in life (ibid.). People often simultaneously experience conflicting feelings (for example, grandiosity and insecurity), and the presence of two opposing ideas doesn't necessarily imply that the system is broken. We need to accept ambiguities in life, to stop trying to control our feelings and, rather, act in accordance with the most functional approach, even if it contradicts our feelings. This chapter presented four skills that DBT targets:

- *Mindfulness:* When you practice setting your attention on the present moment, you develop a more-immediate awareness of feelings, sensations, and thoughts.

- *Distress tolerance:* Practicing mindfulness helps you to accept reality for what it is, without trying to change or adjust it. Accepting reality allows you to tolerate the distress associated with depersonalization and other psychological suffering.

- *Emotion regulation:* Emotion regulation means resisting acting according to what your unpleasant emotions urge you to do. Emotion regulation strategies allow you to tolerate the discomfort associated with *not* doing what depersonalization wants you to do.

- *Interpersonal effectiveness:* Practicing assertive communication with loved ones can help defuse conflicts so that you start to feel less alienated from the people closest to you.

This chapter tailored these DBT skills to the struggles of people with depersonalization. We presented mindfulness exercises to introduce you to the philosophy and practice of mindfulness as it applies to depersonalization. We explored assertiveness as an interpersonal effectiveness skill. We discussed actual dialogue to understand how people with DPD and their family members can use assertive communication.

8

Using Behavioral Strategies

Your feelings, sensations, thoughts, and behaviors more or less make up your experiences. Notice how all but one of these occur completely below the surface, so psychology refers to them as "internal events." Your thoughts, feelings, and sensations are perceptible only to you; no one can share your thoughts with you unless you bring them to the external world through your behavior (such as by speaking or writing your thoughts). This brings us to your only external experience, your behavior. Your behavior is the only thing you can show to the outside world, and it's the only thing you truly have any control over. As discussed in chapter 6, receiving the mere instruction not to think something will cause you to think about it, and you feel a variety of feelings you would rather not feel. The internal world doesn't respond well to instruction. However, your overt behaviors are entirely under your control. Right now you could tell yourself to lift your arm and touch your nose with your hand; likewise, you could tell yourself not to. Your movement is something you have complete control over.

Your control over your behavior is an important leverage point, and one you can use to help you manage and alleviate the suffering associated with depersonalization. You are physically capable of putting yourself in situations that will be good for your overall well-being. Strategies discussed in this chapter will tell you exactly what to do to expose and acclimate yourself to feared or avoided experiences. Discomfort will inevitably arise in this process. So, refer to the strategies discussed in chapters 6 and 7 to help you accept the discomfort.

Behavioral Therapy (BT)

Behavioral therapy has evolved over the years. Today, it generally involves increasing contact with feared situations to increase your tolerance for discomfort. So, for example, a friend who was afraid of spiders avoided them to decrease his discomfort. It worked in the short term, but only encouraged him to avoid spiders and situations related to them in the long term. If there was a spider in his way and he ran from it, his anxiety decreased. However, he realized pretty soon that avoiding spiders limited his activities; he couldn't get near a campsite, go on a picnic, or take a hike in the woods, for example. In fact, during the summer, he was almost unable to go outside at all. You can see how short-term relief of anxiety can result in impairment in life; the long-term consequence of avoidance is isolation and stagnancy. If this person exposes himself to spiders and *doesn't* run away, he'll initially experience extreme discomfort, disgust, and anxiety. However, continued exposure to spiders will eventually evoke a lowered emotional response. The long-term benefit will be the ability to do things in spite of anxiety and other sources of psychological discomfort surrounding spiders, allowing him to go camping, hike, or spend prolonged periods outdoors.

Changes in your anxiety response occur on a neurological level. Basically, your brain sends out distress signals when it perceives something that could potentially be dangerous. Responding to the distress signal by fleeing from whatever makes you uncomfortable will bring much relief, thereby increasing the likelihood that you'll respond this way in the future (for example, if you see a spider and run from it, you'll be relieved and will be more likely to employ this strategy in the future). Neurologically, the response to run away is strengthened. However, if you stay in the situation that makes you uncomfortable and no disastrous consequence occurs, you'll strengthen the response of *not* running away. Once exposed to something that provokes anxiety, your brain will continue to put out the distress signal for some time. But a neurological state of arousal is not one that can be maintained indefinitely. Eventually, your brain will get tired and relax; you'll have no choice but to relax because this process is your brain's natural reaction. Likewise, exposing yourself to your depersonalization experience will eventually cause your brain to adjust, and theoretically, you'll acclimate to the discomfort. Behavior therapy strives to put you into contact with all of the things depersonalization causes you to feel uncomfortable about. Other behavioral techniques put you into contact with things about life that are important to you and reinforcing for you. We'll discuss these strategies next.

Exposure and Response Prevention (ERP)

Exposure refers to coming into contact with things you fear; *response prevention* means preventing avoidance responses that would be dysfunctional for you.

Depersonalization frequently causes people to avoid situations that provoke the depersonalization experience. This may include social situations, professional settings, or mentally taxing activities. If you have depersonalization and you start to feel very alienated during a dinner party, noticing how little you are connecting to the situation and others around you will likely worsen your depersonalization experience. When your feelings about being depersonalized worsen, the pain you feel may intensify to the point of inducing panic. At this point, the avoidance or escape response would be to excuse yourself from the party, thereby relieving the discomfort of alienation. In this example, ERP involves remaining at the dinner party and really allowing yourself to feel the panic that may arise. This sounds simple enough, but ERP can be a bit more complicated than it first appears. The following sections will introduce various ERP exercises.

EXERCISE: Exposure to Traumatic Experiences That Preceded DPD

As mentioned earlier in the book, depersonalization is often preceded by some kind of traumatic incident, such as sexual abuse or a physical trauma, or by use of psychoactive drugs. Referring back to the personal scenarios presented throughout the previous chapters, Emily initially experienced depersonalization after an episode of marijuana use; John acknowledged an early experience with depersonalization following a sports-related injury, though it didn't cause any significant physical trauma; and Danny acknowledged an early history of verbal and occasional physical abuse from his mother. Many people with depersonalization relate having experienced emotional neglect or abandonment by their parents and other caregivers.

Thoughts about traumas and prolonged abuse may bring about feelings of anxiety, disgust, and depersonalization. Behavioral principles tell us that rather than avoid something that makes you uncomfortable, the best thing to do for your well-being is to *go into* the discomfort, really explore it, flesh it out, create elaborate mental imagery about it, and sit with those feelings until they run their course. The best system for doing this is to carefully recount the events leading up to depersonalization, writing them out in a specific and detailed narrative. Once you have written your narrative, pull it out whenever the feelings come over you, reread it, and try to reexperience the feelings. The sample narrative we provide next is what Emily wrote about an incident of marijuana use, after which her awareness of her experiences seemed permanently altered.

Against my better judgment, I said yes when the joint was passed around. My history with pot should have dissuaded me, but I figured it would be okay. I distinctly remember the feeling that came with the inhalation: it cut into my lungs aggressively and had sort of an overwhelming, spicy, tingly, itchy feeling that abruptly hit me. Suddenly my bodily sensations were hijacked. It felt like every molecule in my body was standing on end and rotating quickly. I felt like my body was about to act independently, without my instruction. I was afraid I was going to fall on the floor; I was afraid I was going to be pulled into space; I was afraid gravity would reverse; I was afraid my limbs would abandon my body. It was terrifying. Every time I moved my head or tried to reorient my awareness, I was overwhelmed by the feeling that I'd lost control. So I closed my eyes, curled up on the couch, and tried to block out awareness and ride it out. When I woke up the next day, the feelings of dissociation weren't nearly as bad, but things weren't right. My environment felt unfamiliar, alien. I had trouble taking in a scene; if I was looking at a kitchen, I knew intellectually that that was what I was looking at, but somehow individual parts of the scene didn't fit into a complete whole. This was also how I felt about my body: when I walked, I knew my arms and legs were moving, but it didn't feel as though they were working as part of an integrated whole. I kept waiting for these feelings to dissipate. I felt like there were cotton balls in my brain; the fuzziness felt like TV static humming constantly in the background.

Notice how Emily's narrative describes the experience in a visceral way. This technique is useful because this type of language allows Emily to experience her memories similarly to how she originally experienced them. Writing this type of description will allow you to reexpose yourself to the original discomfort, thereby helping you acclimate to it.

When you write your narrative, be as specific as possible, paying particular attention to your internal experiences (for example, your sensations, feelings, and thoughts). Then when reviewing the narrative, read each sentence and really try to put yourself back into the scene; try to imagine exactly how it felt. This type of narrative works very well for exposing yourself to feelings associated with rape or witnessing a violent act; obviously you can't (nor would you want to) reexperience the original trauma, but imaginal techniques allow you to experience some of the feelings associated with the original event. This allows you to become desensitized to the feelings and move beyond the trauma.

EXERCISE: Exposure to the Disastrous Consequences of Depersonalization

Most people with depersonalization can imagine a disastrous scenario in which depersonalization completely takes over and ravages everything that was previously enjoyable about life. These scenarios can haunt you. Also, in and of itself, depersonalization can become a source of anxiety. But willingness to have feelings of depersonalization and to face the fears surrounding it will allow you to overcome it. In other words, if you are willing to face the potential devastation depersonalization might cause, you'll be less likely to succumb to it. Disastrous consequences are therefore a target for exposure. Similar to the previous exercise, the best way to expose yourself to the disastrous consequences of depersonalization is to write a narrative, or what's sometimes referred to as a *flooding statement*. Basically, the goal is to flesh out the specific fears, making them awful and taking them to an absurd level. Usually these flooding statements end in death, isolation, or physical and emotional agony. Again, the purpose is to face the ultimate worst-case scenario so that your fears about depersonalization no longer control you. Flooding statements are usually phrased in the past tense, to make it sound as though your future self is telling the story retrospectively. Keep in mind that the goal here is not to describe what *does* happen to people with depersonalization but, rather, to blow up your *worst fears* about what *could* happen. The following flooding statement is from Susan, the person with DPD who was introduced in chapter 2. Again, her flooding statement doesn't represent a realistic course for depersonalization, but rather, it inflates her fears about loss of autonomy, her doubt of her control over her actions, and her loss of affection for her loved ones.

Depersonalization just kept getting worse. At first it felt like I was becoming more and more alienated from my husband and children. I reached a point where I felt nothing more for any member of my family than a stranger on the street.

It was around this time that I started to feel like everything I did came from some source outside of me; I started to completely lose my autonomy. Slowly I began to realize that my body was, in fact, moving without my consent. It began slowly, with just the lift of an arm here, a tap of the foot there. But eventually I was having whole conversations that I wasn't in charge of; I was driving to places I had no intention of going to. At first the things I did were more or less what I would do, but as my loss of autonomy got worse, I found that I was doing more and more stuff that disturbed me. I would say nasty things to my loved ones and put myself and others in harm's way by driving in a risky manner.

Depersonalization just kept getting worse, and eventually I felt like I was merely an observer in a tower, looking down on what my body was doing and cringing at the choices "I" was making. I became violent in several situations, when normally I would be able to keep my cool. One time, I was in the parking lot, and a woman bumped into my car with a shopping cart. I flew off the handle, screamed at her, and started hitting her car with a baseball bat in retaliation. All the while, I couldn't stop myself; I could only look on, horrified at my actions.

Several other incidents ensued, and all the while, my grasp on my experiences was collapsing. I found it difficult to integrate information, or even understand where I was or what was happening around me. I thought this must be what Alzheimer's feels like. I couldn't form new memories or remember what my body had been doing earlier in the day. I began to hear about things I had done that I had no memory of, horrible things. Apparently I had attacked my husband, scratching and slapping him. He was going to leave me, declaring that he couldn't take this anymore, that he'd had enough. Furthermore, he was taking the kids. I was going to be completely alone.

It was around this time that my body stopped moving much at all. I found that I no longer had any control over my body and that whatever had been controlling my actions had now ceased. I was beginning to succumb to a sort of numb paralysis. My awareness of sensations was distorted and disintegrated. I can now sort of notice being in a room. Intellectually, I know it's a room, but I can't take in the whole scene at one time. My awareness is foggy and my attention is nonexistent. My family has completely abandoned me due to the tumultuousness of my situation.

*I believe that I'm in a hospital of some sort, and my arms
are restrained. I receive no visitors except people in white
coats. I have virtually no experiences I can retain. My
awareness of my body and every one of my experiences
come in glimpses but are merely fragmented snippets of my
former awareness. Feelings of social alienation have given
way to complete and utter isolation, leaving me more or
less trapped inside my mind, observing my experiences in
a disjointed fashion and having no life to speak of that
exists outside the bed restraints. And what's worse is that
the doctors believe I can live a long life this way. This is all
I have to look forward to forever.*

Many people with depersonalization fear completely losing
control. Susan's flooding statement exposes this fear, providing a
description of the absolutely worst imaginable inflation of this fear.

Compose your own flooding statement. If your greatest fear
about depersonalization is loss of control, try to determine what
really frightens you about that prospect. Is it doing harm? Is it being
at the mercy of forces outside your control? Is it abandonment? If
your fear is loss of social connection, what *really* upsets you about
being unable to connect to people? Is it feeling as though you are
missing out on one of life's greatest joys? Is it losing someone who's
important to you? Is it having no one in your life and becoming a
complete recluse? Really get creative with these stories. This is your
opportunity to go *into* your worst fears to expose them for their
absurdity.

EXERCISE: Interoceptive Cue Exposure

If you had a broken leg, you would feel the pain of it more if you
tried running than if you were lying down. In other words, when
we are engaged with sensations, those sensations will be more

prominent to us. People with depersonalization often try to limit their internal sensations to avoid awareness of their numb feelings. But again, while that may provide relief in the short term, it naturally restricts what you allow yourself to do and consequently limits the richness of your life. That's why *interoceptive cue exposure (ICE)* can be helpful. ICE involves awareness and exacerbation of internal discomforts in order to help restore your awareness. This exposure to the physiological components of arousal (such as increased heart rate and blood pressure, and shortness of breath) can also be helpful because it will shift attention from the anxiety and other psychological discomfort that depersonalization has you all wrapped up in.

Following is a list of interoceptive cue exposures you can practice to increase your flexibility so that you experience a variety of unpleasant or alienating physical sensations. As you read over the list, keep in mind that your safety is the most important priority. Don't participate in an activity that you believe you may not be able to do safely (such as extreme exercise if you have a heart condition). Be sure not to do anything in the interest of exposure to extreme sensations if it will cause you physical harm, because self-induced physical harm will not only be physically unsafe but also counterproductive to your psychological health.

- Stand outside in the cold or heat for an extended period.

- Induce panic symptoms by:

  - holding your breath as long as you can;

  - sprinting around the block to get your heart rate up, increase your blood pressure, and induce shortness of breath;

  - straining your muscles to increase blood pressure;

- hyperventilating.

- Take a shower that's a bit too cold or too hot.

- Fill a sock with screws and nails, tie it closed, and rest it on your hand, noticing any sensations that occur to you and how the sensations change over time.

- Hold an ice cube for as long as you can.

- Kneel on a broomstick.

- See how long you can tolerate listening to really loud music.

- Throw a pot on the floor to hear the loud noise it produces.

- Slam doors—again, to hear the loud noise.

- Eat something you don't like.

- Suck on a lemon.

- Deliberately smell something you find unpleasant.

See if you can think of any extreme sensations you would typically resist, and give them a try, too. Notice that exposure activities are all aimed toward increasing your flexibility and tolerance so you can experience a range of sensations, including unpleasant ones.

EXERCISE: Exposure to Extreme Emotions

Depersonalization can sometimes arise in response to extreme emotional experiences, as discussed throughout this book. Therefore, exposure to extreme emotions may allow you to become desensitized to them, thereby increasing their tolerability. Next are some suggested activities, but don't limit yourself to this list. You know better than anyone what types of things arouse intense emotions in you, so give it some thought and come up with some additional activities on your own.

- Watch emotionally evocative movies—tearjerkers, violent imagery such as rape and murder scenes, or scary movies—and notice what emotions are inspired.

- Have a loved one *practice* saying critical or upsetting things to you. This is not an opportunity for your loved one to take out frustrations or air grievances. Rather, you'll choose exactly what your loved one will say, in an effort to inspire extreme emotions; then your loved one will recite the phrases verbatim.

- Listen to angry or sad music for an extended period.

- Look at photo albums.

- Watch home videos of you and your loved ones. This type of activity tends to inspire bittersweet feelings, which is a good thing; don't try to distance yourself from the discomfort that arises as a natural conse- quence of caring about things.

- If you are an animal person, go to a pet store and give some love to a furry creature. The whole point is to feel something you can experience intensely.

Exposure to Feared Situations

Other important avenues for exposure are concrete things, or people in your life who tend to inspire feelings of depersonaliza- tion and consequently have been neglected or abandoned. Suppose chronic DPD led you to drop out of school, and now imagining being in an academic situation inspires incredible fear. This is the ideal exposure challenge. You can regard all anxiety- and depersonalization-inducing things as therapeutic exercises; imagine that your exposure exercises are merely practice.

If you really think about it, certain situations are more associated with depersonalization than others. Make a list of activities, places, scenarios, people, or settings that tend to inspire depersonalization, and then rank them from 1 (no depersonalization, no need to avoid) to 10 (very extreme depersonalization, always avoid), according to how strong your urge to avoid them is:

Activity, Place, Scenario, Person, or Setting That Tends to Inspire Depersonalization	Strength of Urge to Avoid (1–10)

This table represents your hierarchy of feared activities. Start with the easy ones and start making contact. Get yourself into the situations, and will yourself to experience the emotional consequence no matter what it is. Don't judge whatever reaction you have during this exercise; just be willing to experience it. At some point during one of these exposure exercises, you may have an urge to flee, to get out of the situation and neutralize your discomfort. Notice how you can have that urge but not act on it. Notice how your will and the corresponding action of your muscles have ultimate authority about what you'll allow yourself to experience. Using the mindfulness and willingness strategies explored in chapters 6 and 7, notice how your mind chatters at you when you're doing something unpleasant. It may say things like, "Wow, this is uncomfortable. I just want to leave," "I can't stand this anymore," and "This exercise is stupid." Notice how your mind responds to everything and that you aren't necessarily required to act on your mind's "two cents' worth" about the situation. Getting back into contact with things that make you uncomfortable, whether it be social activities, mentally taxing exercises, or contact with certain people, will allow you to start getting back into life. A rich life is full of things that are pleasant and unpleasant. Having depersonalization, you've been dealt a particularly rough hand, but this doesn't mean you won't be able to live a rich existence.

Behavioral Activation

Behavioral activation is reengaging in things in life that are enjoyable or otherwise reinforcing for you. As is often the case when depersonalization interrupts your life, you have probably found that things hold less joy for you than they used to. Now's the time to get back into those things, even if your heart's not in it. The whole theory behind behavioral activation is that, often, people who are experiencing any sort of psychological problem become completely overwhelmed by psychological dysfunction. Some people who are depressed spend all day in bed, which reinforces their depression;

people who really care about social acceptance to the point where they become very anxious in social situations don't wind up having any social experiences; people with depersonalization want to feel something so badly that they lose contact with all the things that used to make them feel. Though an ironic tendency, it's a very real obstacle to recovering from any psychological disorder. Fortunately, this tendency provides you with an important leverage point for treatment: even if you don't feel like doing something you used to enjoy, do it anyway, and, hopefully, eventually you'll find it rewarding in some way.

Make a list of hobbies, activities, day trips, and other things you found enjoyable at one time in your life. Then plan to *do* them. Schedule times for these activities and write them on your calendar. Don't let yourself off the hook when the time comes; hold yourself accountable, and consider this a necessary step in your recovery process. Again, even if you don't feel like it, do it. If you really make time and do these things, your life will become richer as a consequence. Your life will come to stand for more than just depersonalization.

1. _____

2. _____

3. _____

4. _____

5. _____

6. _____

7. _____

8. _____

SUMMARY

Behavior therapy involves interacting with things, emotions, and sensations you find uncomfortable. A variety of experiences may elicit depersonalization, for example, traumatic events and extreme emotions. Exposure to depersonalization and other unpleasant emotions and sensations will allow you to desensitize yourself to the discomfort. If you are willing to endure the discomfort associated with depersonalization, you'll be able to do anything that might contribute to a richer life.

We introduced exposure and response prevention exercises that involve exposure to:

- extreme emotions;

- intense physical sensations;

- any underlying trauma that may be associated with depersonalization;

- things or events that tend to bring about feelings of depersonalization;

- feared disastrous consequences of depersonalization.

We also explored behavioral activation, as a way to increase contact with enjoyable aspects of life. People with depersonalization often feel uninspired by things that were previously enjoyable. The aim of behavioral activation is to get reinvolved in hobbies, activities, and goals that were once important to you. The purpose is to "fake it till you feel it," allowing behaviors to precede enthusiasm in the hope that enthusiasm will follow.

9

Other Treatment Options

This book has focused primarily on acceptance and behavioral techniques to treat depersonalization. Other options are available, and we'll describe a sampling of alternatives in this chapter. A detailed explanation of these options is beyond the scope of this book, but two other books have been written for people with depersonalization, focusing more specifically on some of these additional treatments. *Feeling Unreal: Depersonalization Disorder and the Loss of the Self*, by Daphne Simeon and Jeffrey Abugel (Oxford University Press, 2006), provides an excellent introduction to the contemporary understanding of depersonalization. We'll briefly introduce cognitive-behavioral strategies next, but if you're interested in further study, refer to *Overcoming Depersonalization and Feelings of Unreality*, by Anthony S. David and colleagues (Constable and Robinson, 2007), which is a self-help book that explores cognitive-behavioral therapeutic strategies for managing depersonalization.

Other Psychological Approaches

We explored acceptance and behavioral strategies in the previous four chapters. Some people find that acceptance strategies resonate more than other ones, and vice versa. This is highly individual, and studies have yet to fully flesh out who responds to what type of therapy and why. The best thing for you, as a person with depersonalization, to do is to try each of the different approaches and see which strategy reaches you the most.

Cognitive Behavioral Therapy

There are a few ways in which traditional cognitive behavioral therapy (CBT) differs from the acceptance approaches we've focused on up to now. Acceptance emphasizes the importance of accepting relentless, troubling thoughts, whereas CBT basically involves changing your thinking patterns to change how you feel. The assumption is that distorted thinking contributes to disordered behaving and emotional suffering. Traditional CBT makes reference to "underlying assumptions" and "core beliefs" that contribute to our most difficult psychological struggles (Beck 1976). Common assumptions and beliefs for people with depersonalization include:

- "My feelings of unreality are intolerable; I can't live like this indefinitely."

- "I'll be able to have a rich life only if I can make these feelings go away."

- "I must have some sort of brain damage."

- "I'll be rejected by my family once they realize I feel numb toward them."

- "I have no personality."

- "People notice how messed up I am."

You could subject these beliefs to empirical evaluation; would they, in fact, hold up if you looked at the evidence? Cognitive strategies seek to answer such questions. Theoretically, realizing that your thought is exaggerated or inaccurate takes some of the emotional punch out of it. Then, conceivably you'll be able to replace inaccurate thoughts with more accurate interpretations. We'll explore this technique next.

EXERCISE: Examining the Evidence and Finding Alternative Interpretations

CBT emphasizes the importance of charting emotional experiences to identify thinking patterns that might be involved. This entails recognizing thoughts that occur to you automatically when you encounter emotionally upsetting situations. You then subject each thought to an examination of the evidence. If the automatic thought is exaggerated or inaccurate, you generate an alternative interpretation, equipping yourself with a logic-based belief rather than an emotionally guided one. Following is an example of a thought record completed by Susan, one of the people with DPD, who was introduced in chapter 2. Use the following format as a template to create your own thought record.

Date	Situation	Emotions	Automatic Thoughts	Evidence	Alternative Interpretation
Describe actual event leading to the unpleasant emotions, or the stream of thoughts leading to them.	Specify sad, anxious, angry, and so on, and rate degree of emotion (0–100); 0 = low, 100 = high.	Write automatic thoughts that preceded emotion. Rate belief in them (0–100%).	Look for any concrete information that confirms or denies your automatic thought.	Write another way of seeing the situation. Rate belief in alternative interpretation (0–100%).
5/19	I was at a party, met a bunch of new people, and couldn't remember their names.	Panic: 60	I must have early-onset Alzheimer's disease. 60%	Though my memory and concentration don't seem as good as they used to be, early-onset Alzheimer's is very rare. I have no other symptoms and had previous neurological tests that revealed nothing abnormal.	Memory and concentration difficulties may be related to DPD. Plus, my nervousness in the situation likely contributed. 70%

5/20	My husband hugged me, and I didn't feel anything for him.	Depression: 70	My DPD's getting worse; I'm going to be vegetative eventually. 70%	It's not always "getting worse." My DPD log shows me that over the past few months, my overall level of depersonalization hasn't changed significantly. Plus, DPD doesn't cause people to become vegetative.	I have better days and worse days. Today I feel particularly dissociated. 80%
5/22	The new medication I'm taking doesn't seem to be working. This is basically the only class of medication I hadn't tried yet.	Disappointment: 60 Desperation: 80	I'm never going to feel like myself again. This life isn't worth living. 70%	There's no evidence that I'll never feel like myself again. Many aspects of my life are still rewarding.	I'm disappointed about the latest medication failure. I don't know what the future holds and that's scary, but there's no sense in fortune-telling. 80%

While many of Susan's observations were accurately unpleasant, her automatic thoughts seemed to consistently highlight a worst-case scenario. She seemed to read her experiences according to the worst possible thing that could happen, rather than what's most likely to happen. Many people who use the thought record technique find that looking at things in terms of "most likely" rather than "most awful" takes some of the sting out of negative thinking. As you practice these techniques, you get better at identifying distorted thinking and quickly generating a more moderate interpretation.

Common Thought Distortions

Next are some common cognitive distortions as they relate to depersonalization. As you read through them, see if you can think of examples of distortions in your own thought patterns.

All-or-Nothing Thinking: You may believe you'll never be able to find happiness again if you can't get rid of numbness, and that life will be completely unrewarding. (That said, it's common for people with chronic DPD to indicate that it's invalidating to call this belief a "distortion," because the discomfort is so constant and unyielding that it's virtually impossible to appreciate the positive experiences that contradict the overall negative experiences.)

Overgeneralization: "I can never feel anything" might be an example of overgeneralization for someone with DPD. Basically, if you feel generally numb, but not numb to absolutely everything, this statement is an overgeneralization and is likely somewhat inaccurate.

Mental Filtering: If depersonalization is particularly distressing on a given day, it's very easy to reflect on the recent past in terms of how bad depersonalization has been lately. Because your mind is inherently negative, your mental filter tends to show you only information that fits your negative interpretations.

Disqualifying the Positive: Let's say that yesterday you actually enjoyed a movie or a meal, but you woke up today feeling more disconnected. It's easy to forget about the positive experiences when you also have memories of negative experiences.

Jumping to Conclusions: "I'm never going to feel better" would be an example of jumping to conclusions. There's no way for any of us to tell how we'll feel or what we'll experience in the future, so this is a distortion because it's an unknown. Remember, CBT is all about learning how to base your beliefs on what evidence suggests.

Magnification and Minimization: "The pain of DPD is unbearable" is an example of magnification. While the pain truly feels unbearable, it's *not* unbearable, because every moment you sit in your skin, you are bearing it. It's more accurate to say something to the effect of "This pain is truly consistently uncomfortable."

Emotional Reasoning: It's easy to imagine that because you feel something, it must indicate something external. If you feel hopeless, things must be hopeless; if you feel numb toward your spouse, you must not care about people or connectedness; if you feel overwhelmed in social settings, there must be something wrong with your brain or there must be something legitimately threatening about the situation. Letting your emotions guide your interpretations doesn't always lead you to the most functional outcome.

Making "Should" Statements: "I'm twenty-three years old. I *should* be able to work" is a "should" statement that Emily made at one point during her treatment. This is focusing on how things should be based on some arbitrary set of rules, rather than on what the situation actually is. If you think about it, there's no absolute truth for how to be a human being, and concentrating on the many ways in which your experience doesn't live up to what it *should* be won't do you any good.

Labeling and Mislabeling: It's easy to see yourself as "depersonalized," as though that defines who you are as a whole. This is an unhelpful belief because it may urge you to always act according to depersonalization.

Personalization: "I am a complete disappointment. My parents punished me for this and I started to feel depersonalized," might be a good example of personalization. Even though we tend to be harsh critics of ourselves, it's very hard to trace the causes of psychological suffering. While your relationship might feel very real to you, these attributions aren't necessarily always accurate.

You may be upset that we're suggesting that, in some ways, your thinking is what's making you feel miserable. As implied previously, cognitive distortions can sometimes have a pejorative ring to people. It's pretty invalidating to say that your suffering is at least partially influenced by your own "irrational" ways of seeing the world. And even though your thoughts about depersonalization may be exaggerated at times, your acknowledging that doesn't necessarily make the feelings any easier to tolerate. That said, some people find it very calming to identify inaccurate thinking. If you can identify your thoughts and learn to change them, then you are in control of changing your feelings. Of course, you can also just take control of your life by seeing your thoughts as mere thoughts, and living your life according to your values, the acceptance-oriented approach we suggested in earlier chapters. However, you now have two strategies of approaching thoughts. A treatment will be most useful to you if you buy into it, so review the different approaches and see which rings true for you. But we suggest not trying to control your thoughts and not giving such importance to them.

Wellness

Though wellness isn't really a psychological treatment, it's often a psychological goal. Essentially, wellness prioritizes self-care, health, diet, routine, exercise, sleep, hygiene, and enjoyable activities, because they contribute to and enhance your psychological well-being. You already know how to do this; your grandmother told you—and her grandmother told her—things like, "Early to bed, early to rise…," "An apple a day…," "All work and no play…," "Eat your vegetables, there are starving people in _____," and "Eat your spinach." We've all heard these adages. But wellness supports psychological health, whether you suffer from alcoholism, depersonalization, schizophrenia, depression, or anything else.

The best way to incorporate a wellness routine is to be systematic about it. Scheduling your day in advance can be very powerful for instituting changes in your routine. If you've planned in advance to do something, you are more likely to do it. While this isn't an infallible rule, the first step to making change is planning change.

Psychopharmacological Options

No pharmacological treatment has been found to work indefinitely for depersonalization. The drugs discussed next were found to bring about mild to moderate improvement in some to approximately half of the people with depersonalization who participated in drug trials (Simeon and Abugel 2006). While that sounds pretty wishy-washy and a little bit dismal, often, finding an effective medication cocktail requires some trial and error for people who experience chronic depersonalization. It's important to be patient when seeking what works to alleviate some of the discomfort associated with depersonalization, and to keep in mind that depersonalization symptoms seldom go into full remission. Many of the pharmacological options aim more to relieve the *symptoms* of depersonalization rather than the syndrome itself. For example, depression is a common secondary symptom that's likely to be treated using an SSRI (discussed later). People with depersonalization also commonly tell of having obsessive thinking about internal experiences; Anafranil (clomipramine) or another tricyclic medication, as well as the newer SSRIs or SNRIs, may be prescribed to combat obsessive thinking. People also frequently experience panic or extreme anxiety in conjunction with DPD, so a benzodiazepine may be prescribed to address compounding anxiety. Loss of concentration may be treated with a stimulant. The point is, only a few drugs target the dissociative symptoms per se; the others target the resulting discomfort.

Selective Serotonin Reuptake Inhibitors (SSRIs)

Selective serotonin reuptake inhibitors (SSRIs) are a good place to start for depersonalization treatment. SSRIs work by increasing absorption of serotonin (a neurotransmitter that regulates mood) in the brain. The newest class of antidepressants, they have been found effective for a wide range of mood and anxiety conditions. But SSRIs are prescribed for everything from smoking cessation to fibromyalgia, indicating that sufficient absorption of serotonin affects many aspects of our comfort. SSRIs have been found effective for treatment of the depression frequently experienced by people with depersonalization. For reasons not entirely known, some people with DPD also find relief from the dissociative symptoms.

Anafranil

Anafranil (clomipramine) is a *tricyclic* antidepressant. Tricyclics are a bit older than SSRIs and have a greater number of side effects. For that reason, they're sometimes prescribed when SSRIs don't work. However, some studies have shown that Anafranil may be slightly more effective for treating obsessive thinking than comparable SSRIs. Whether it's obsessive self-focus, obsessive thinking about potential brain damage, or other frightening explanations for discomfort, obsessive thinking is a central feature of DPD. A drug that targets this process may provide some relief from secondary obsessive thinking for people with depersonalization.

Benzodiazepines

Xanax (alprazolam), Klonopin (clonazepam), Ativan (lorazepam), and Valium (diazepam) are all medications in the benzodiazepine drug class. *Benzodiazepines* are antianxiety drugs, or *anxiolytics*, that have been prescribed for years for anxiety conditions such as panic disorder, obsessive-compulsive disorder, generalized anxiety disorder, and social phobia. Benzodiazepines induce physiological relaxation (relaxation of muscles, slowed heart rate, and sedation). Depersonalization can arise due to a prolonged period of excessive anxiety; because benzodiazepines diminish autonomic arousal, the dissociative symptoms may also diminish. Another interpretation is that the experience of depersonalization provokes anxiety, and benzodiazepines relieve this secondary symptom that causes a great deal of discomfort.

Naltrexone

Naltrexone is an opioid antagonist, meaning that it blocks the reception of opiates in the brain. You're probably asking, "What does that have to do with my feelings of depersonalization?" Opiates can produce a numbing effect that may bring about feelings of depersonalization. In fact, giving certain opiates to people without DPD causes a brief period of depersonalization. Known opiates are heroin, morphine, and other such chemicals. Naltrexone helps a person to withdraw from these opiates, so if opiates can trigger depersonalization, then anything that works against opiates can perhaps stop the depersonalization. While the exact reason for this isn't exactly clear, the effectiveness of naltrexone for DPD suggests that the body's response to pain and stress is somehow involved in the development of depersonalization. Investigation into the effectiveness of opioid antagonists is in a preliminary stage. Undoubtedly, as study of pharmacological treatments for DPD becomes more advanced, more light will be shed on the use of this class of medications.

Magnetic Stimulation

Transcranial magnetic stimulation (*TMS*) is an experimental treatment that has gained recent attention for treatment of depersonalization (Jiménez-Genchi 2004). People with depersonalization participated in weekly sessions of exposure to weak transcranial electrical stimulation induced in the tissue by rapidly changing magnetic fields. Basically, electrical currents are applied to the head (non-surgically) and stimulate targeted areas of the brain. Like most treatments for depersonalization, the benefit is modest, but it's a noninvasive procedure with minimal reported side effects.

Cingulotomy

A more invasive option has gained recent attention for use on chronic, debilitating, and drug-resistant OCD, namely, *cingulotomy*. Cingulotomy has also been proposed as a treatment for depersonalization. Essentially, it involves surgically damaging neurological structures involved in emotional processing (specific regions of the anterior cingulate cortex). This region associates emotion centers of the brain with higher-order or executive functioning (frontal lobe areas). Basically, the rationale behind this procedure is that obsessive thinking can result from approaching emotional dilemmas using areas of the brain that are responsible for solving problems. Theoretically, if these different areas of the brain are not free to correspond as easily, obsessive thinking will be more manageable. Due to the obsessive nature of depersonalization, cingulotomy is considered a possible treatment for severe, pervasive, and drug-resistant depersonalization.

It's very important to understand that this is extremely experimental at this time. Psychosurgery is generally considered a last resort, because it's incredibly invasive and has unpleasant cognitive side effects, and there's no telling whether the treatment will actually work for a particular person. Many people who have undergone this procedure have indicated difficulty concentrating and remembering things, as well as other cognitive and physical difficulties, after the procedure, so consider this option only as the last resort.

SUMMARY

This chapter explored a few additional treatment considerations. Traditional cognitive behavioral therapy (CBT) techniques are used successfully for depersonalization. We also introduced specific thought observation and disputation techniques. We listed common cognitive distortions that are consistent with a traditional CBT understanding of depersonalization. We suggested wellness as an adjunct to any psychological treatment, because attention to your bodily needs and self-care is generally associated with overall psychological well-being.

This chapter also briefly explored pharmacological options. Medication of depersonalization often emphasizes treating the symptoms rather than directly treating the dissociation. Antidepressants may alleviate secondary depression or discomfort associated with DPD, stimulants may help the cognitive symptoms, and benzodiazepines may alleviate secondary anxiety. We also explored the importance of finding an effective combination of drugs.

A couple of experimental treatments, including transcranial magnetic stimulation and cingulotomy, were explored, as well as the rationale and risks for each. Because medical and surgical treatments for depersonalization are still in a formative stage, it's fair to say that there's room for growth.

10

Frequently Asked Questions

What are the symptoms of depersonalization? Symptoms of depersonalization include subjective feelings of unreality, feeling detached from your mental or physical activities, feeling mentally "foggy," experiencing "numb" feelings for people and subjects you previously had passion for, and being very distressed by these experiences.

What are the common triggers of depersonalization? No one thing is the definitive cause of depersonalization. Some people develop chronic DPD randomly, while others can point to specific incidents that caused the perceptual shift. Common triggers include extreme short-term trauma (such as surviving a horrific accident), prolonged trauma (such as childhood sexual abuse), long-term exposure to exhausting conditions (such as working eighty-hour weeks for twenty years), and chronic or even isolated drug use. Many people with DPD say they had their first experience of depersonalization during and following marijuana use; a few other drugs may also be responsible, including ketamine (also known as "Special K"). It's fair to deduce that triggers may be either psychological or chemical. With regard to psychological triggers, one rule predominates: the more intense the traumatic incident, the less exposure is needed to trigger depersonalization. Likewise, the less traumatic an incident, the longer a person would need to be exposed to develop DPD. For example, being held at gunpoint for thirty seconds may be enough to trigger depersonalization, whereas you might have to endure extreme work stress for years to bring about DPD.

How can DPD affect my life? In addition to making you feel awful, DPD can impair the quality of your life quite a bit. Many people with DPD begin to avoid situations or people that bring about unpleasant feelings, including depersonalization. You may neglect previously pleasurable activities (such as intimacy, going out with friends, or participating in mentally challenging activities). Your relationships may suffer, and your work responsibilities may seem impossible. For these reasons, DPD wreaks havoc on previous functioning.

What is acceptance and commitment therapy? Acceptance and commitment therapy (ACT) is part of the "third wave" of behavioral therapy. The third wave uses strategies of acceptance to help you live according to what's actually important to you, rather than what your discomfort urges you to do. This approach involves finding ways to accept discomfort that comes up along the way in life. ACT may be especially useful for treating depersonalization because much of your life with depersonalization involves taking discomfort with you while staying engaged in life. Chapters 5 and 6 explore this approach in depth, and discuss how to apply acceptance strategies to live a more balanced life despite depersonalization.

How does willingness relate to acceptance? Acceptance and willingness go hand in hand; to accept unpleasant feelings, you need to be willing to experience things that are bound to make you uncomfortable. So for example, if social situations tend to elicit depersonalization for you, your willingness to go into social situations despite this will lead to accepting discomfort. Ultimately, acceptance is behavioral; if you're willing to feel pain, you won't get as easily pulled into the pursuit of feeling better and will, thus, be more accepting of discomfort.

What is mindfulness? Mindfulness relates to staying in the moment and concentrating only on your immediate awareness, rather than getting carried away by your mind's reactions to your experiences. Mindfulness may be useful for treating depersonalization, because depersonalization often involves failure to pay attention to all of your experiences (for example, you may be tragically aware of your depersonalization experience, but you probably haven't paid attention to the feeling of the fabric that currently touches your skin or the sound of cars driving by). Mindfulness, grounding, and retraining your attention all refer to this general approach.

Is acceptance of chronic discomfort truly possible? Many people struggle with the idea that they need to accept the truly awful discomfort they have to endure in life. Plus, some people are more like the biblical Job than others; sometimes truly awful circumstances fall into your lap, and it may seem as if you are being targeted more than the average person. Life's not easy, and your life with depersonalization is particularly hard. Accepting your depersonalization may also be difficult to do. That said, you're still here; this is your time on earth, right now. Making the most of that involves trying to accept the hand you've been dealt. It's not easy, but the reward of trying is reciprocally reinforced. In other words, the more you try, the more you get out of life; and the richer your experiences, the more you want to continue trying. This process will hopefully lead to finding some kind of peace in your predicament, whatever that may be.

What is dialectical behavior therapy (DBT)? DBT is another "third wave" behavior therapy using acceptance-oriented strategies. The purpose is to override emotion-guided urges that wouldn't be good for you in the long run. For people with DPD, this would likely include urges to avoid things that increase their depersonalization experience. The core skills taught in DBT include mindfulness, distress tolerance, emotion regulation, and interpersonal effectiveness. Together, these tools facilitate personal growth and help you to be more deliberate in your behaviors, while validating your emotional reactions.

What is cognitive behavioral therapy? Cognitive behavioral therapy (CBT) involves changing negative or irrational thinking patterns so you can feel better. CBT strategies include systematically disputing troubling thoughts, that is, looking at them for their accuracy and replacing exaggerated or inaccurate thoughts with more rational responses. The rationale is that if you can see the world in a more objective light, you'll feel more comfortable in situations you previously avoided.

What is behavioral therapy? Behavioral therapy (BT) involves participating in activities you may usually avoid because they are unpleasant or have unpleasant side effects. The theory is that if you can "face your fears" (or discomfort or tension), your mind and body will become habituated (or used) to the discomfort, and the discomfort will eventually become more tolerable. Behavioral therapy strategies include exposure to feared things, situations, or ideas, as well as participating in life activities that are meaningful to you (such as going to the movies with a friend or going on a date). BT is all about doing; even if you aren't into life or aren't enjoying it, go ahead and do it, and according to behavioral principles, you can't help but improve your life.

Can traditional cognitive behavioral therapy and acceptance approaches be used in together? Yes and no. There are certain theoretical points that make the different approaches mutually exclusive. However, from a practical standpoint, it's possible to tap into both approaches to cope with depersonalization. Some people find the cognitive strategies very reassuring and useful when overriding unhelpful emotional impulses, while some people find the acceptance concepts very comforting. There are no rules here; find what works for you, and don't be afraid to try new things. The good news is that behavioral therapy is consistent with both acceptance therapies and traditional CBT, so make sure that you are doing your life while you are learning new ways to approach your thoughts and feelings.

What can my family members do to help? So frequently, family members want to make sure they are doing the right things to facilitate their loved one's recovery. This can be exceptionally difficult, because the loved one's feelings are so wrapped up in the family members' feelings, and vice versa, often leading to fighting, which is usually unproductive. It's important for family members to keep in mind that it's impossible to force someone to stop having psychologically dysfunctional patterns.

Another specific thing your family members can do is validate your suffering. It's important for people with depersonalization to know that others acknowledge how painful DPD can be. Often, family members resort to accusation and frustration, and while this is an understandable response, it's not helpful in the long run. These concepts were briefly introduced in chapter 7 under the heading "Interpersonal Effectiveness."

Finally, because there's so often an overlap between depersonalization and obsessive-compulsive symptoms, certain family-oriented therapies that are useful for the OCD population may be useful for families of people with DPD. For example, philosophical obsessions, or focus on human existence, the autonomy of your actions, and so on may lead you to seek reassurance from family members. While this may relieve anxiety in the short term, it's likely to reinforce DPD rather than make it go away in the long run. So it's a good idea for family members to try to refrain from giving reassurance, while remaining supportive and empathic.

Depersonalization and multiple-personality disorder are both considered dissociative. How do these disorders differ? Multiple-personality disorder (contemporarily referred to as dissociative identity disorder, or DID) involves the development of one or several alter egos, or distinct, fractured personalities. Like DPD, DID can be brought on by extreme trauma. Both disorders are dissociative in that they make it more difficult for you to relate to your own experiences. DID may represent the extreme end of dissociation, while DPD may represent a milder reaction. Rest assured that most people with DPD will not develop DID; DID is relatively rare, even among people with DPD.

If I've been diagnosed with DPD as well as another psychological condition, how do I know which disorder a given symptom is related to? How do I know which therapy is best for which disorder? DPD is characterized by a subjective feeling of being outside yourself, feelings of unreality, difficulty feeling connected to other people, subjective concentration or attention difficulty, obsessive focus on the autonomy of your actions, and feeling cognitively "fuzzy" or "foggy." Other psychological symptoms may be better explained by a comorbid (co-occurring) condition. But it's important to keep in mind that diagnosis is mainly useful in helping you to feel a sense of community and to understand your struggles. It also helps mental health professionals understand how you are suffering and how to help. However, what's most important is for you to target the specific areas in life you would like to change and the specific behaviors you would need to change to make those life changes. Generally, you don't need to know what diagnosis is responsible for which behavior to do this. It's possible to simply target the behaviors.

It's also common for people with depersonalization to become incredibly preoccupied with their diagnosis. And while this is a noble pursuit, it may become an obsessive process. This is why it may be more useful to focus on the behaviors you would like to change than on what disorder is responsible for those behaviors.

Why did I get depersonalization? Many people ask whether depersonalization develops as a result of genetics, environmental factors, or even some sort of pathogen. Like many psychological conditions, depersonalization develops because people who are predisposed to dissociation are exposed to certain environmental factors that bring the syndrome about. Everyone has a way of responding to extreme discomfort, stress, or trauma. Some people may be more likely to develop OCD, some become significantly depressed, some become vulnerable to extreme emotional volatility, some experience flashbacks related to trauma, and some have no unpleasant psychological reaction. There's no telling exactly how a person will respond to extreme psychological discomfort. Based on your unique genetic makeup and specific environmental conditions, you have found yourself with depersonalization. Unfortunately, because you can't change your genetics and you can't change the past, there's no way to instantly relieve your suffering. You can overcome depersonalization by specifically targeting its behavioral symptoms, challenging yourself, and being willing to experience discomfort, as this book describes.

What's the prognosis? Though attention on DPD research has increased in recent years, there's still a dearth of empirical data on the condition. While specific prognosis figures are unavailable, DPD seems to follow one of a few different courses: acute depersonalization may endure for some time, allowing it to be labeled as chronic, but then go away unexpectedly; chronic depersonalization may remain indefinitely, leading to major life impairments; or finally, depersonalization may remain but become less pronounced and more manageable. Treatment, whether pharmacological or psychological, will improve the prognosis, as a few studies have indicated (Simeon 2004; Hunter et al. 2005). Again, more research is needed to clarify uncertainties.

Does DPD ever make you "lose your mind"? No. People with depersonalization have a subjective sense of unreality. The operative word here is "subjective." This means that your reality testing is intact; you can still distinguish reality, but your feeling of reality is impaired. You aren't losing your mind, nor will DPD make you lose your mind. Sometimes it may feel as though your awareness of reality is getting worse, but again, this is subjective and is not associated with legitimate impairments in reality testing or cognitive functioning. It suffices to say that most people with DPD feel or fear that they are losing their minds, but no one ever does. Therefore, DPD causes you to *fear* the loss of mental control, but it does not cause you to actually lose mental control.

Will episodic depersonalization lead to chronic depersonalization? Episodic depersonalization doesn't necessarily lead to chronic depersonalization. Episodic depersonalization is something that many people experience throughout the course of a lifetime. Such episodes are generally brief and isolated to a period of traumatic experience.

Do I have a neurological disorder? Technically, DPD is not a neurological disorder, in that specific neurological mechanisms are functioning normally. Brain imaging does sometimes reveal anomalies in information processing in certain people with DPD, but the brain itself is functioning properly.

Can I have a good relationship with my family despite my having DPD? There's no reason why you won't be able to create a good relationship with your family. It's possible to maintain healthy relationships while you overcome the symptoms.

Is DPD hereditary? Are there things I should consider before having children? Genetic factors aren't yet known, but improvements in genetic research emerge every day. It suffices to say that genetic traits provide each person with the propensity to develop certain psychological characteristics. Whether each person does or doesn't develop those characteristics depends on environmental factors. Trauma is a common environmental precipitant for DPD, as well as just about every other psychological condition. So don't let DPD guide the decision of whether or not to have children, because too many factors other than genes have likely contributed to your having developed depersonalization.

Is it a good idea for me to date? Difficulty with interpersonal connectedness is a common symptom. Panic and discomfort over your DPD experience may make you fearful of engaging in social situations and meaningful relationships, but you don't need to act on such fears. Exposure to social situations will help you acclimate to the discomfort of depersonalization, so dating is advisable.

If I can connect to one or two people, does that mean I don't have DPD? Not necessarily. Because you naturally experience different kinds of connections with different people, it's likely you'll have varying degrees of depersonalization with different people in your life.

What if I can connect to animals, but not people? Do I have DPD? Possibly. Many people with depersonalization feel a strong connection to animals but not people. It's not entirely clear why this is so.

Are there medications that help with DPD? Antidepressants, anxiolytics, and opioid antagonists are frequently prescribed to help people cope with symptoms of depersonalization, but a pharmacological cure is still unavailable.

Is there a cure? There's no cure. We recommend seeking psychological treatment that will allow you to manage the symptoms and lead a valued life.

Will people shy away from me if I reveal my DPD? While it's not necessarily kind or right, psychological disorders often carry a stigma. Many people with DPD choose to select whom to reveal their struggles to. This is your right. However, it's probably best to let your closest loved ones in on the diagnosis, because they, too, are likely struggling as a result of your DPD. An open dialogue will allow for movement and communication on all fronts.

Will loved ones think I can't have feelings for them? Sometimes loved ones need to be reassured of your feelings for them. If you are, in fact, having difficulty re-creating feelings for someone you previously loved, perhaps this is an issue to explore with your therapist. Reminding your loved ones that you have unclear feelings about them would likely just cause more conflict rather than solve the issue.

How can I be successful in life with DPD? Behavioral therapy can provide strategies that will allow you to be successful in life while managing the discomfort associated with DPD.

What's the age of onset for DPD? Age of onset varies for DPD, but it generally develops during adolescence to middle age.

Will I grow out of DPD? The course of DPD varies and is highly individual. Some people's symptoms inexplicably and abruptly go away, some people live with reduced symptoms, and some people suffer with DPD for many years. However, therapy and medication can help.

Do women get DPD more frequently than men? Generally, prevalence rates among men and women are comparable.

Are there any support groups, websites, or other forums out there for people with DPD and their families? Many websites and online forums are available for people with DPD, including:

- Depersonalization Support Community—
  www.dpselfhelp.com

- Depersonalization Home—depersonalization-home.com

These sites are primarily run by people with DPD, and they can offer valuable remote support. Our own website often cites new research, and offers support groups and helpful suggestions:

- Bio Behavioral Institute—
  www.biobehavioralinstitute.com

Can someone who experiences mental or physical detachment feel anything or even cry? People with DPD often feel things intensely. The predominant symptom among people with DPD is despair about the emotional detachment they feel or the perceptual disconnection that interferes with information processing. The absence of emotion is not really the problem; rather, people with DPD describe having the tragic realization that their connection to their emotions is somehow disrupted.

A website program said it could cure my DPD with CD therapy for a payment. Should I trust this? No. Many of these websites misrepresent their products. There's no easy or instant cure for depersonalization, and it's important to be wary of any organization that makes such claims.

When do depersonalization symptoms actually become a disorder? Symptom clusters (symptoms that tend to occur together) are generally classified as disorders if they cause either marked distress or marked impairment. Only a mental health professional with experience treating DPD should determine whether or not you meet diagnostic criteria for DPD.

What's the prevalence of depersonalization disorder? Depersonalization disorder affects between 1.7 and 2.4 percent of the population (Hunter, Sierra, and David 2004).

Does depersonalization disorder affect cognitive functioning? People with depersonalization may have more difficulty with tasks requiring maintained attention. One study found that people with DPD had more difficulties than average with immediate visual and verbal recall of material (Guralnik et al. 2007).

Is cognitive behavioral therapy (CBT) an effective treatment for people diagnosed with depersonalization disorder? CBT does work for treatment of DPD. One study found that 29 percent of people no longer met criteria for DPD diagnosis after receiving CBT (Hunter et al. 2005).

How do I explain DPD to my family? Your loved ones may benefit from reading this book or other books on DPD. Fortunately, resources are now available to shed a bit more light on the condition you struggle with, and it's useful for everyone involved to be as informed as possible. *Feeling Unreal: Depersonalization Disorder and the Loss of the Self*, by Daphne Simeon and Jeffrey Abugel (Oxford University Press, 2006), is a comprehensive introduction to DPD that both you and your family will find helpful.

How do I find a qualified behavioral therapist? Depending on where you live, finding a therapist with experience in treating DPD using behavioral strategies may be difficult. Furthermore, if you are working with your insurance company, your options will be even more limited. If you can't find a therapist with a specialty in DPD, find a behavioral therapist with experience in treating anxiety disorders. Be sure the therapist you choose practices exposure and response prevention (ERP) and behavioral activation. Ask questions about how the therapist conducts therapy, because your success in treatment depends on the type of treatment you receive. Finally, how well you bond with your therapist is of vital importance. If, after a few visits, it doesn't seem like a good fit, don't be afraid to discuss this openly.

I'm in behavioral therapy with a therapist who understands DPD. How long will I have to be in treatment? It's uncertain how long you will need to be in treatment. Length of treatment depends on your goals, your level of functioning, and other variables. Session frequency will also determine how quickly you start to see results. To best assess your progress, make sure you consistently review your goals with your therapist.

How will I know if my treatment is working? If you're experiencing improvements in functioning and mood, you are probably benefiting from treatment. Getting back into life, pursuing things you value, and feeling more peaceful are indications of progress.

Can brain damage cause depersonalization? DPD, if properly diagnosed, is not caused by brain damage. Before a mental health professional diagnoses DPD, a neurological evaluation should be conducted to rule out neurological explanations for your symptoms.

Is it possible that what I'm experiencing is early-onset Alzheimer's, rather than DPD? This is a very common self-diagnosis among people with DPD. Again, a neurological evaluation will rule out any underlying neurological conditions. However, once alternative explanations have been ruled out, it's important to redirect your focus away from them, because speculating about this can become an obsessive, unproductive process.

Neurologically, what causes the experience of depersonalization? It's important to note that there are no *structural* abnormalities in the brains of people with DPD (the shape and size of the brain is normal, and no areas are damaged or atrophied). There are a few *functional* abnormalities in the brains of people with DPD (the way the brain processes information and integrates reality). Specifically, the brains of people with DPD show abnormal processing of visual, auditory, and somatosensory information, as well as prefrontal processing of emotional experiences (Medford et al. 2005). In other words, neuroimaging has confirmed that people with DPD have a difficult time integrating sensations and emotions.

How is depersonalization related to panic? Depersonalization may actually be an adaptive strategy your brain applies to cope with intense emotional reactions. Depersonalization may sometimes represent the extreme end of intense feelings, such as panic. If your brain acknowledges intense discomfort, it may numb you to that discomfort. However, this is only one explanation, and it may oversimplify the problem.

Can medication for depersonalization actually make it worse? This is an unfortunate catch-22 for people with depersonalization. Inward self-focus can actually make DPD worse, and the best way to get you to focus on your internal experiences is to give you a pill that might make you feel better. When you are given a new medication, what do you do? You monitor your feelings for signs of improvement, which only sensitizes you to your experience of depersonalization. The best way to handle this is to give new medications time to work; don't let your initial experiences with a new medication determine whether or not it's working. Of course, this doesn't mean you should ignore potentially serious side effects (such as a rash). Make sure you relay all of your experiences to your psychiatrist, and keep in mind that you may have to ride out the initial sensitization that may occur.

What's the difference between depersonalization and philosophical obsession? Some people with OCD have obsessions about philosophical issues, such as the meaning of life and the nature of reality. This overlaps with depersonalization, because many people with depersonalization are led to doubt the autonomy of their actions, for example, asking things like, "How do I know that I'm really responsible for what my body does?" People with depersonalization may actually *feel* as though their actions aren't under their control, while people with philosophical obsessions may just be plagued by thoughts about them. It's a fine line, and as discussed in chapter 4, DPD and OCD occur together quite a bit.

What's the most important thing I can do to improve my situation today? Even though it feels awful, get up at a reasonable time, eat balanced meals at appropriate times, consider your doctor's recommendations about medication, and try to fill your time with productive activities that contribute to feelings of competence. It sounds simple enough, but this can be immensely difficult for someone who's suffering with depersonalization. The strategies discussed in this book will help you tolerate the discomfort associated with living a psychologically healthy lifestyle in spite of your DPD.

Recommended Reading

David, A., D. Baker, E. Lawrence, M. Sierra, N. Medford, and E. Hunter. 2007. *Overcoming Depersonalization and Feelings of Unreality: A Self-Help Guide Using Cognitive Behavioral Techniques*. London: Constable and Robinson.

Epstein, M. 1999. *Going to Pieces Without Falling Apart: A Buddhist Perspective on Wholeness*. New York: Broadway Books.

Haddock, D. B. 2001. *The Dissociative Identity Disorder Sourcebook*. New York: McGraw-Hill.

Hayes, S. C., and S. Smith 2005. *Get Out of Your Mind and Into Your Life: The New Acceptance and Commitment Therapy.* Oakland, CA: New Harbinger Publications.

Kabat-Zinn, J. 1990. *Full Catastrophe Living: Using the Wisdom of Your Body and Mind to Face Stress, Pain, and Illness.* New York: Delacorte Press.

McKay, M., J. C. Wood, and J. Brantley. 2007. *The Dialectical Behavior Therapy Skills Workbook: Practical DBT Exercises for Learning Mindfulness, Interpersonal Effectiveness, Emotion Regulation, and Distress Tolerance.* Oakland, CA: New Harbinger Publications.

Simeon, D., and J. Abugel. 2006. *Feeling Unreal: Depersonalization Disorder and the Loss of the Self.* New York: Oxford University Press.

References

Altman, N. 1995. *The Analyst in the Inner City: Race, Class, and Culture Through a Psychoanalytic Lens*. Boca Raton, FL: The Analytic Press.

American Psychiatric Association (APA). 2000. *Diagnostic and Statistical Manual of Mental Disorders (DSM-IV-TR)*. 4th ed. Text rev. Washington, DC: American Psychiatric Association.

Baker, D., E. Hunter, E. Lawrence, N. Medford, M. Patel, C. Senior, M. Sierra, M. V. Lambert, M. L. Phillips, and A. S. David.

2003. Depersonalisation disorder: Clinical features of 204 cases. *British Journal of Psychiatry* 182:428–33.

Beck, A. T. 1976. *Cognitive Therapy and the Emotional Disorders.* Madison, CT: International Universities Press.

Bodnar, S. 2004. Remember where you come from: Dissociative process in multicultural individuals. *Psychoanalytic Dialogues* 14 (5):581–603.

Bromberg, P. M. 1996. Standing in the spaces: The multiplicity of self and the psychoanalytic relationship. *Contemporary Psychoanalysis* 32:509–35.

Butler, L. D., and O. Palesh. 2004. Spellbound: Dissociation in the movies. *Journal of Trauma and Dissociation* 5 (2):63–88.

Cardeña, E., and D. Spiegel. 1993. Dissociative reactions to the San Francisco Bay Area earthquake of 1989. *American Journal of Psychiatry* 150 (3):474–78.

Cassano, G. B., A. Petracca, G. Perugi, C. Toni, A. Tundo, and M. Roth. 1989. Derealization and panic attacks: A clinical evaluation on 150 patients with panic disorder/agoraphobia. *Comprehensive Psychiatry* 30 (1):5–12.

Cohen, E. 2007. Enactments and dissociations driven by cultural differences. *American Journal of Psychoanalysis* 67 (1):22–9.

Curran, H. V., and C. Morgan. 2000. Cognitive, dissociative, and psychotogenic effects of ketamine in recreational users on the night of drug use and 3 days later. *Addiction* 95 (4):575–90.

Dixon, J. C. 1963. Depersonalization phenomena in a sample population of college students. *British Journal of Psychiatry* 109:371–75.

Feigenbaum, J. J., F. Bergmann, S. A. Richmond, R. Mechoulam, V. Nadler, Y. Kloog, and M. Sokolovsky. 1989. Nonpsychotropic cannabinoid acts as a functional N-methyl-D-aspartate receptor blocker. *Proceedings of the National Academy of Sciences* 86 (23):9584–87.

Guralnik, O., T. Giesbrecht, M. Knutelska, B. Sirroff, and D. Simeon. 2007. Cognitive functioning in depersonalization disorder. *Journal of Nervous and Mental Disease* 195 (12):983–88.

Harper, M., and M. Roth. 1962. Temporal lobe epilepsy and the phobic anxiety-depersonalization syndrome: I. A comparison study. *Comprehensive Psychiatry* 3 (3):129–61.

Hayes, S. C., and S. Smith. 2005. *Get Out of Your Mind and Into Your Life: The New Acceptance and Commitment Therapy.* Oakland, CA: New Harbinger Publications.

Hayes, S. C., K. D. Strosahl, and K. G. Wilson. 1999. *Acceptance and Commitment Therapy: An Experiential Approach to Behavior Change.* New York: The Guilford Press.

Horowitz, K., S. Weine, and J. Jekel. 1995. PTSD symptoms in urban adolescent girls: Compounded community trauma. *Journal of the American Academy of Child and Adolescent Psychiatry* 34 (10):1353–61.

Hunter, E. C., D. Baker, M. L. Phillips, M. Sierra, and A. S. David. 2005. Cognitive-behaviour therapy for depersonalisation disorder: An open study. *Behaviour Research and Therapy* 43 (9):1121–30.

Hunter, E. C., M. Sierra, and A. S. David. 2004. The epidemiology of depersonalisation and derealisation: A systematic review. *Social Psychiatry and Psychiatric Epidemiology* 39 (1):9–18.

Ilechukwu, S. T. C. 2007. *Ogbanje/abiku* and cultural conceptualizations of psychopathology in Nigeria. *Mental Health, Religion, and Culture* 10 (3):239–55.

Jacobs, J. R., and G. B. Bovasso. 1992. Toward the clarification of the construct of depersonalization and its association with affective and cognitive dysfunctions. *Journal of Personality Assessment* 59 (2):352–65.

Jiménez-Genchi, A. M. 2004. Repetitive transcranial magnetic stimulation improves depersonalization: A case report. *CNS Spectrums* 9 (5):375–76.

Kinzie, J. D., W. H. Sack, R. H. Angell, S. Manson, and B. Rath. 1986. The psychiatric effects of massive trauma on Cambodian children: I. The children. *Journal of the American Academy of Child and Adolescent Psychiatry* 25 (3):370–76.

Kluft, R. P. 1993. Multiple personality disorders. In *Dissociative disorders: A clinical review*, ed. D. A. Spiegel, 17–44. Lutherville, MD: Sidran Press.

Krystal, J. H., J. D. Bremner, S. M. Southwick, and D. S. Charney. 1998. The emerging neurobiology of dissociation: Implications for treatment of post-traumatic stress disorder. In *Trauma, memory, and dissociation*, ed. J. D. Bremner and C. R. Marmar, 321–64. Washington, DC: American Psychiatric Press.

Linehan, M. M. 1993a. *Cognitive Behavioral Treatment of Borderline Personality Disorder*. New York: The Guilford Press.

———. 1993b. *Skills Training Manual for Treating Borderline Personality Disorder*. New York: The Guilford Press.

Mathew, R. J., W. H. Wilson, N. Y. Chiu, T. G. Turkington, T. R. Degrado, and R. E. Coleman. 1999. Regional cerebral blood flow and depersonalization after tetrahydrocannabinol administration. *Acta psychiatrica Scandinavica* 100 (1):67–75.

McVey-Noble, M. E., S. Khemlani-Patel, and F. Neziroglu. 2006. *When Your Child Is Cutting: A Parent's Guide to Helping*

Children Overcome Self-Injury. Oakland, CA: New Harbinger Publications.

Medford, N., M. Sierra, D. Baker, and A. S. David. 2005. Understanding and treating depersonalisation disorder. *Advances in Psychiatric Treatment* 11:92–100.

Montagne, B., M. Sierra, N. Medford, E. Hunter, D. Baker, R. P. C. Kessels, E. H. F. de Haan, and A. S. David. 2007. Emotional memory and perception of emotional faces in patients suffering from depersonalization disorder. *British Journal of Psychology* 98 (pt 3):517–27.

Nuller, Y. L., M. G. Morozova, O. N. Kushnir, and N. Hamper. 2001. Effect of naloxone therapy on depersonalization: A pilot study. *Journal of Psychopharmacology* 15 (2):93–95.

Penfield, W., and T. Rasmussen. 1950. *The Cerebral Cortex of Man: A Clinical Study of Localization of Function.* 1st ed. New York: Macmillan.

Phillips, M. L., N. Medford, C. Senior, E. T. Bullmore, J. Suckling, M. J. Brammer, C. Andrew, M. Sierra, S. C. R. Williams, and A. S. David. 2001. Depersonalization disorder: Thinking without feeling. *Psychiatry Research* 108 (3):145–60.

Phillips, M. L., and M. Sierra. 2003. Depersonalization disorder: A functional neuroanatomical perspective. *Stress* 6 (3):157–65.

Pizer, S. A. 1998. *Building Bridges: The Negotiation of Paradox in Psychoanalysis.* Hillsdale, NJ: The Analytic Press.

Rufer, M., S. Fricke, D. Held, J. Cremer, and I. Hand. 2006. Dissociation and symptom dimensions of obsessive-compulsive disorder: A replication study. *European Archives of Psychiatry and Clinical Neuroscience* 256 (3):146–50.

Seligman, R., and L. J. Kirmayer. 2008. Dissociative experience and cultural neuroscience: Narrative, metaphor, and mechanism. *Culture, Medicine, and Psychiatry* 32 (1):31–64.

Sierra, M. 2008. Depersonalization disorder: Pharmacological approaches. *Expert Review of Neurotherapeutics* 8 (1):19–26.

Sierra, M., and G. E. Berrios. 2001. The phenomenological stability of depersonalization: Comparing the old with the new. *Journal of Nervous and Mental Disease* 189 (9):629–36.

Sierra, M., C. Senior, J. Dalton, M. McDonough, A. Bond, M. L. Phillips, A. M. O'Dwyer, and A. S. David. 2002. Autonomic response in depersonalisation disorder. *Archives of General Psychiatry* 59 (9):833–38.

Simeon, D. 2004. Depersonalisation disorder: A contemporary overview. *CNS Drugs* 18 (6):343–54.

Simeon, D., and J. Abugel. 2006. *Feeling Unreal: Depersonalization Disorder and the Loss of the Self.* New York: Oxford University Press.

Simeon, D., O. Guralnik, E. A. Hazlett, J. Spiegel-Cohen, E. Hollander, and M. S. Buchsbaum. 2000. Feeling unreal: A PET study of depersonalization disorder. *American Journal of Psychiatry* 157 (11):1782–88.

Simeon, D., O. Guralnik, M. Knutelska, R. Yehuda, and J. Schmeidler. 2003a. Basal norepinephrine in depersonalization disorder. *Psychiatry Research* 121 (1):93–97.

Simeon, D., E. Hollander, D. J. Stein, C. DeCaria, L. J. Cohen, J. B. Saoud, N. Islam, and M. Hwang. 1995. Induction of depersonalization by the serotonin agonist meta-chlorophenylpiperazine. *Psychiatry Research* 58 (2):161–64.

Simeon, D., M. Knutelska, D. Nelson, and O. Guralnik. 2003b. Feeling unreal: A depersonalization disorder update of 117 cases. *Journal of Clinical Psychiatry* 64 (9):990–97.

Svedin, C. G., D. Nilsson, and C. Lindell. 2004. Traumatic experiences and dissociative symptoms among Swedish adolescents: A pilot study using Dis-Q-Sweden. *Nordic Journal of Psychiatry* 58 (5):349–55.

Wellenkamp, J. 2002. Cultural similarities and differences regarding emotional disclosure: Some examples from Indonesia and the Pacific. In *Emotion, disclosure, and health,* ed. J. W. Pennebaker, 293–312. Washington, DC: American Psychological Association.

Wikan, U. 1990. *Managing Turbulent Hearts: A Balinese Formula for Living.* Chicago: University of Chicago Press.

Wilson, K. G., and T. DuFrene. 2008. *Mindfulness for Two: An Acceptance and Commitment Therapy Approach to Mindfulness in Psychotherapy.* Oakland, CA: New Harbinger Publications.

Yule, W., O. Udwin, and K. Murdoch. 1990. The "Jupiter" sinking: Effects on children's fears, depression, and anxiety. *Journal of Child Psychology and Psychiatry* 31 (7):1051–61.

Fugen Neziroglu, Ph.D., ABBP, ABPP, is a board-certified cognitive and behavior psychologist involved in the research and treatment of anxiety disorders, obsessive-compulsive spectrum disorders, trichotillomania, hoarding, body dysmorphic disorder, and hypochondriasis at the Bio Behavioral Institute in Great Neck, NY. She is coauthor of *Overcoming Compulsive Hoarding* and many other books. Her books have been translated to various languages.

Katharine Donnelly, MA, is a behavior therapist at the Bio Behavioral Institute in Great Neck, NY. Her areas of interest include behavioral and acceptance-oriented therapies and obsessive-compulsive spectrum behaviors.

Foreword writer **Daphne Simeon, MD,** is associate professor of psychiatry at the Albert Einstein College of Medicine in New York City. She is director of the depersonalization and dissociation program at the Beth Israel Medical Center in New York.

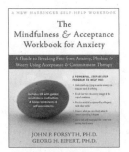
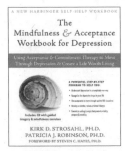